The Life of Katherine Mearl Murdoch Lyon

Katie in 1944, her eighteenth year.

The Life of Katherine Mearl Murdoch Lyon

Katherine Mearl Murdoch Lyon

WAKING LION PRESS

ISBN 978-1-4341-0425-0

Published by Waking Lion Press, an imprint of The Editorium

Waking Lion Press™, the Waking Lion Press logo, and The Editorium™ are trademarks of The Editorium, LLC

The Editorium, LLC
West Jordan, UT 84081-6132
wakinglionpress.com
wakinglion@editorium.com

Contents

Autobiography	1
My Life: Stories and Lessons	13
Childhood and Growing Up	13
Young Adulthood	29
Adulthood	51
Life Lessons, Family Heritage, and Other Topics	69
Fashion Show	87
Interview with Leah Anderson, Granddaughter	97
Ethnicity Estimate from Ancestry DNA	109
Favorite Recipes	111
Poor Man's Sauce, Hot Fudge Topping	112
Chili Sauce	113
Cereal Nibbles	114
Mustard Sauce, Maddox Dressing	115

Carmel Sauce, Carmel Sauce—Robin	116
French Dressing, Salad Dressing Mix (Hidden Valley)	117
English Toffee, Peanut Brittle	118
Golden Fudge, Sugared Popcorn	119
Fudge, Pecan or Peanut Brittle	120
Almond Joys, Peanut Honey Balls (Peanut Butter Cups)	121
Grandma's Salad	122
Cranberry Salad	123
Goulash	124
Pine Tree Salad	125
Carrot Cake	126
Rhubarb Crunch	127
Meat Loaf, Ann Landers Meatloaf	128
Applesauce Fruitcake	129
Sweet and Sour Pork	130
Chinese Chicken and Rice Big and Little	131
Snickerdoodles	132
Sweet and Sour Chicken	133
Sugar Cookies (Buttermilk), Cherry Delight	134
Filled Raisin Cookies, Pecan Diamonds	135
Pumpkin Cookies, Toll House Cookies	136
Pecan Tarts	137

*Crunchy Bumpy Munchy Cookies (Ranger Cookies),
Sour Cream Sugar Cookies* 138

Rocky Road Brownies, Milk Chocolate Brownies . . 139

Date Spin Wheel Cookies 140

Molasses Sugar Cookies 141

Old Cookie Cookies, Nonstick Rolled Butter Cookies 142

Chocolate Marshmallow Cookies 143

Pinapple Coconut Cookies, Chocolate Chip Cookies . 144

Photo Gallery 145

Autobiography

Well, here goes. I was born at Farnum, Idaho, August 5, 1926, to Brigham and Luann Hammon Murdoch. They named me Katherine Mearl Murdoch after my Aunt Kate Hicken and Mearl Murdoch, my sister-in-law.[1] I was the tenth child of five boys and five girls. I grew up in a loving family. My mother was forty and my father was fifty-five when I was born. We lived on a farm at Farnum, overlooking Fall River, with a beautiful view of the Tetons.

I loved playing with my cousins, Uncle Tom's kids, who lived a mile up the road. They were the only close relatives we had living nearby. We would see our other Murdoch relatives when they came for reunions. I remember seeing my Aunt Tress and Aunt Kate only once, also Uncle Dave.

My mother and dad worked so hard. My first memories of Dad are of him in bed with rheumatic fever. Mother and Howard and Wallace took care of the cattle, milked the cows, and delivered the calves and lambs. At times Mother washed her clothes on the board, sometimes in a washer outside that had a foot and hand lever that I could work. It was fun, but I was afraid of the wringer.

Dad plowed the fields with horses, and sometimes I would walk

---

1. Daughter Kathy identified Mearl as the wife of Katie's older half-brother, Rue.

with him as he walked behind the plow. I liked to ride on the drill. We never had much money, and Mother made butter and sold it to buy our groceries. I thought everyone was equal in financial matters, and I guess we were. We were all poor. The depression was on, and they had a very hard time.

It was always fun when the married siblings and their families came for Sunday dinner. I loved all my nieces and nephews and spent a lot of time playing with them. I spent a lot of time exploring the farm, sometimes alone and sometimes with Wallace. I liked to hunt for bird nests, but we weren't allowed to take the eggs out. I don't know how Mother raised ten kids on the river without losing one or two. Wallace and I spent a lot of time playing in the canal and the river. We went barefoot a lot. We snared squirrels and rode horseback. I never really learned to like horses.

I went to school in a two-room schoolhouse. I started when I was seven. I had to stay in with Dad while Mom did the chores, so I was a year late. I really think they thought I was too little. There were three kids in my first-grade class, Dewayne Schofield, Gilbert Murdoch, and I. My teacher was Winifred Kirkham. In the second grade, Mrs. Smith thought I should be with the kids my own age, so she put me in the third grade. There were Myrth and Melvin Benson, Keith Whittle, and Jack Whitmore.

When I was in the fifth grade, Dad and Mom bought a house in Ashton and started a dairy. We lived across the street from Tom and Alta. Their place was like a second home. I don't know how they ever survived three teenagers hanging around all the time. I will always be grateful for the love they gave us, and they were both a big influence in my life.

All through school, my best friend was Rose Marie Whittemore. We did everything together. We were happy, crazy, fun-loving teenagers, and she meant a great deal to me.

Autobiography

Farnum School

When I was sixteen I started working at the City Drug Store. This was a really fun time for me. I got over being bashful and started dating boys. I had lots of boyfriends. They were all good kids, mostly, and we had an awful lot of fun. I graduated in 1944. I always worked and earned my own money. World War II had started. This was an awful time and an exciting time. All the young men went to war, including Howard and Wallace. Mother hung two stars in her window. It was so hard for my parents to see their sons go. Howard went to Europe and Wallace mostly stayed in Texas. I went to visit him there and met Pauline, whom he later married. I wrote to them both very religiously and also wrote to several guys.

Ben Brower came home on furlough, and we started dating. I thought he was very nice. We kept writing, and when he came home again, before he went overseas, we became engaged. Our romance was mostly through the mail. He was killed on Okinawa by a sniper's bullet. His mother now hung a gold star in the window. So many of our local men didn't come back. I hated the war.

There was a great rejoicing when peace came. A huge crowd gathered on Main Street, and we danced and laughed and cried.

In February 1946, Glade Lyon came home from the war, and we started dating. Howard and Wallace came home too. Glade and I had fun courting. We did lots of things together and really fell in love. Wallace and Pauline were married in May, and Howard and Grace in June. Glade and I were married on December 1, 1946.

It was post-war, and things to buy weren't too plentiful. We didn't have any money anyway. We lived with Glade's parents for a few months, and then we found an apartment. Glade helped his folks in the store. Both our dads were ill. They died six weeks apart in June and July, 1947. Our mothers both had a great loss.

Glade spent his whole life in the store, and I worked when needed, sometimes a lot and sometimes not too much. On June 10, 1951, our first child, Jack, was born. He was named after his Grandfather Lyon. We waited a long time for him, so we really loved him. It was fun being a mother, and I got to stay home and take care of him. We built our new home on top of the basement where we had been living. Glade helped build it, and we spent much time planning it. We always had a nice garden, flowers, and lawn. I loved working in the yard, like my mother.

On July 24, 1953, Suzanne was born, and what a beautiful baby she was. Jack had rheumatic fever at this time, and he was sick so much.

Katie in front of the City Drug Store. The framed star in the window indicates that the store owners had a family member fighting in World War II.

Katie and Glade, bride and groom. Katie picked a black dress just because she liked it.

It left him with a heart murmur. He also had asthma, which always scared us to death. We loved being a family and took the kids everywhere. Sometimes we left them with either of their grandmothers, but I never liked leaving them with baby-sitters. Robin was born April 2, 1957. She was dark with big brown eyes. She really fit in. Everywhere I took her, people commented on how beautiful she was. Kathy came along October 3, 1961. Each baby brought more joy. Kathy was good and never gave us any trouble, even after she was older.

I always had a church calling. I taught Junior Sunday School for ten years straight. I taught Primary and Relief Society. Of all the callings I had, the ones that I enjoyed most were as counselors in the Primary and the Relief Society. I probably liked Relief Society best, but I sure worked hard sometimes. Banquets, hobby night, fundraisers—we had lots of those. Glade and I were sealed in the temple in March 1962. We were really one family now.

Glade worked hard in the store with his mother. They worked side by side for many years. I always ran Toyland in the basement every Christmas season, and we went to Market in Salt Lake City three or four times a year.

My mother died in 1962. She lived such a good life, loving her children and grandchildren. She bore her burdens without complaint. She had great difficulty walking in her last years, but she hoed every weed in her garden on crutches. I will always miss her.

Our kids grew much too fast. They were good students and got good grades. Jack was very musical and played in a band. He played the piano, organ, guitar, trumpet, and harmonica. They could all sing, and we all loved to sing together, travelling or sitting around the campfire.

We always took one trip a year with our kids. We got a travel trailer, and when we outgrew it, we got another, and then another.

We went to California, Minnesota, Pennsylvania, Canada, and several trips to Oregon. We loved the ocean at Newport. Glade and I travelled to Europe in 1965.

Jack attended Ricks College and BYU, and there he met Anne Williams from Ohio, and they were married in September 1972. They have blessed us with four grandchildren, Rebekah, John, Matthew, and Rachel. He is managing editor of Deseret Book Company, and he and Anne have a lovely home in West Valley City.

Suzanne attended BYU and met Larry Hamilton from California. Larry is an engineer for REA, the local electric company. They have three children, Ryan, Aaron, and Wren. Suzanne teaches sixth grade in Ashton and is working on her Master's Degree at this writing. Ryan just left for North Carolina on a mission for the Church. He is our first to go, and we are so proud.

Robin married Verl Miller from Chester. They have two sons, Cody and Scott. They later divorced, and she married Rodolfo Rivas of Mexico. They have two daughters, Maria and Melanie. Rodolfo is a logger, and Robin runs a Day-Care. We are so lucky to have these two families live so close to us.

Kathy attended BYU and met and married Steve Anderson from Oregon. They have four children, Katie, Leah, Joseph, and Gary. Number five is on the way. Steve is an engineer and works as a civilian employee for the Navy. They live in Bremerton, Washington.

Glade and I spent our whole lives working in the American Legion and Auxiliary, serving in all offices many times at local, district, state, and national levels. We attended many conventions and made so many wonderful friends from everywhere.

Glade's mother, Gloy, had dinner with us almost every Sunday. We were together holidays and picnics. She loved her grandchildren and then her great-grandchildren. She filled a mission in California and Arizona and spent many years alone after Jack's death. One time she taught Ryan, Cody, and Scott religious lessons in her home, and she always had refreshments. Her health began to fail. She had pneumonia several times and never really got over it. She spent her last three months with us and died in our home in 1989. Her children and grandchildren presented the program at her funeral.

Glade and I were fortunate to be able to travel a lot. We went to Mexico many times and traveled extensively with Jim and Sadie Harrell and other friends. We grew to love Mexico, the people and the food. Glade's cousin Velda and her husband, Noel Hill, have been a great part of our lives. We have eaten so many meals in their home, and they in ours. We have played cards together forever. The best part was going camping with them every year out in the desert to hunt sage hens. The sage hens were delicious, but the love and friendship we have shared have been very special.

We have such a close circle of friends: John and Ruth Blackburn, Jean and Hugh Hammond, Snick and June Misseldine, Jim and Sadie Harrell, Kiefers, Tighes, Mandellas, Bingos. They are all like brothers and sisters. I wish everyone could have such friends.

Since retirement, Glade has sold real estate with Jim Harrell. He has enjoyed this very much. He always has to be busy. Somewhere, sometime, I started making quilts. I love to sew on the sewing machine. I made all my girls' clothes, and now I piece quilts in my old age. I like to hand-piece, and quilting them is great therapy. I give them all away. I have never counted them, but every year I made a top for the Relief Society. My kids all have several, and I have made one for every grandchild when they got married. May my love always enfold someone.

In October 1992, my sister Martha was diagnosed with cancer, so we brought her home to stay with us. It was so hard for her to

Relaxing after hunting sage hens in the desert at Camas Creek.

leave her home and sons and come here. She was with us for six months. We tried to make her last months as happy and comfortable as we could. We felt much love and compassion for her. We took her home to Cascade to bury her. My sister Tressa helped me much in caring for her.

Blanche, Reed, and Tom have also passed away. We miss them all so much. My brothers and sisters were all a great influence, and I love each one for the contributions they made in my life. I have always enjoyed a special relationship with my sisters Jean and Tressa. At age ninety, Dallas is our patriarch, and we love to visit with him and Agnes.

"The Point" has been a big part of our lives. The two acres we own on Fall River is the meeting place for family gatherings al-

Autobiography

Campfire at the Point.

most every weekend, weather permitting, It's the place for family reunions, the camping place for visiting relatives. We baptized several of our kids there.

Many songs have been sung around the campfire, and thousands of wieners and marshmallows roasted. We have planted hundreds of trees. It's a beautiful place we all love, and Glade works so hard to keep it that way. Life has been so good to us. I am so grateful to have such a good husband and wonderful children and grandchildren to share it with.

My Life: Stories and Lessons[1]

Childhood and Growing Up

Where were you born?

I was born in Farnum, Idaho. Farnum doesn't even exist now. They were just farms five miles out of town. I was born on a farm, in my mother's bedroom. There were no hospitals! She had ten kids, and they were all born at home.

Where do you fit into those ten kids?

I was the youngest.

Did you like that, or was it hard?

Well, it wasn't hard. I'm sure I was spoiled. I'm the only one that didn't have to milk cows, and I hate cows to this day. We had cows and horses and chickens, and all that, besides hay.

---

1. Prepared by Kyleen Ellgen and Christina Folsom. Sponsored by Heidi Higgins, M.S., Department of Psychology, Brigham Young University—Idaho.

Baby Katie in the family garden at Farnum.

What was your favorite thing or chore to do on the farm?

Gathering eggs. But when I was ten, we moved to town, and so I wasn't a farm kid anymore. I had a brother just older than me, and I don't know what we didn't do. And nobody cared. We'd go down to the river. It was so cold! It was Fall River, and it'd fill with snow, so it's always cold. And we'd go down to the river, and we'd build dams, and it's a wonder we didn't drown, because I was little. It was before I was ten! We just had so much fun. I remember my brothers would let me go squirrel hunting with them. They had squirrel traps everywhere, and I'd go with them to gather squirrels. I could kill a squirrel just like they did. I didn't, but it's what I grew up with, so it's okay. We had wonderful neighbors, we knew them all.

What are you parents' names?

Brigham and Luanne Murdoch. Utah is where the Murdochs came from. Murdochs were a big bunch of people. I've found some Murdochs here, which really amazed me.

Which parent did you have the closest relationship to?

Well, I think most every girl is closest to her mom. I remember her swatting my behind really good with a willow. My dad didn't do that. My dad, he was born into a polygamist family. There were two wives. I never did see them; they both died before I was born, but I heard stories all my life. My dad and his brother Tom always had a house next to each other. They got property by homesteading, but you had to live on it. They rode horses from Utah to Farnum to start a farm. My Uncle Tom was kind of fat. And every time he came, I had to put my arms around him and measure him, to see

Katie's parents, Luanne and Brigham Murdoch, all dressed up to go somewhere.

if he got any bigger. And you know, he never got mad. He let me measure him.

Were you a troublemaker? What were your favorite activities as a child?

No, I was just a normal kid. I loved to be in plays. I got little parts, because I was little. They put on plays all the time, and I loved being in those.

What are your siblings' names?

Blanche, Dallas, Reid, Tom, Jean, Tress, Mart, Howard, Wallace, Katie. There's only two living now. My brother Wallace, he lives in Pennsylvania. I never get to see him. I call him on the phone, or he calls me, and that's about it. He's just two years older than me. That's probably why there's just the two of us. My oldest sister had three kids older than me!

Did you grow up playing with your nieces and nephews? Was that strange for you at all?

Oh, yes. I remember the oldest one saying, "Now don't you dare call me aunt." She didn't want me calling her aunt. It wasn't weird; everybody did it.

Are any of your nieces and nephews still alive?

Oh, I have a lot of them. The four oldest ones are dead.[2]

---

2. The children of Katie's oldest sister, Blanche.

The Murdoch family, east of the family home. Left to right. Bottom row: Katie, Luanne, Brigham, Wallace. Middle row: Jean, Blanche, Tressa, Martha, Reid. Top row: Howard, Dallas, Tom.

Have you lived near Rexburg your whole life?

Well, ninety years I lived in Ashton. Ten of it was on the farm, but now it's all a part of Ashton.

Did you like moving to town, or were you sad leaving the farm?

It didn't matter to me.

Which sibling do you think you had the closest relationship with?

I love my sister Jean. She was also into quilting. I loved them all. My oldest brother lived to be 101. I don't really want to live that long, but I don't want to leave my kids. You don't have any choice.

Why do you hate cows so much?

Because I had to herd the stupid things. We took them to town. We had them in a barn in the winter, and during the summer we'd take them out to pasture. We moved them past people's farms; we had about two and a half miles to move them. We had to take the cows out of town and through people's yards. We had horses when we were on the ranch, but we didn't take them to town. I loved the farm. I loved the town too.

What did your father do for a living?

They ran a dairy. He was a bishop for years. In fact, he was the one who built the church. He was fifty years older than I was.

Did your mother work outside the home?

She milked cows, and she drove horses. She had a baby in between. I remember once, my brother and I had a bowl of cereal, and we

Farnum Ward building.

were short of our milk that morning. We both went out to the milk house, and we both wanted some milk for our cereal. My mother said, "Honey, we're short. You can't have milk this morning." Oh, and then she cried, because, she couldn't even have any milk for her own kids. We had maybe eight milk cows. I don't know. Maybe I'm wrong.

Did you have a nickname growing up?

Katie was my nickname. Katherine is my full name. My aunt Kate had a nickname too; she was Katherine, and I was named after her.

Did you have a short haircut as a child?

Yes. It was dark brown. My mother wouldn't let me have it long, and girls didn't have long hair like they have today. I have a brother that went bald. Bless his sweet heart, he went bald, and his hair was brown. It was light brown. He was the lightest. I don't know how come he went bald. He went really bald after he got older. He was the only one. The other brothers had a high forehead, let's put it that way.

How you always gotten perms your whole life?

Yes, since I was a little girl.

Did you have a best friend growing up? What was her name?

Oh, I sure did. Rose Marie. We were inseparable. This was after we came to town, and we did everything together. I was a year ahead of her, and I worked; then after she finished high school she went to nursing school. From then on, we drifted apart, because she moved away. She's still alive too, but I don't talk to her very often. I don't have her number, and I guess she's got a cell phone, and I don't have it. We loved each other. We did everything together.

What kinds of things did you do together?

Just walk to school. Things like that. We were good kids.

How long were you in school for?

I graduated. It was a half mile away. When we lived on the farm, it was a mile and a quarter. We didn't have snow suits; I'd wear

Katie on the farm, embarrassed because her brothers have dressed her in boys' clothes. Note the buggy and sheep camp in the background.

my brother's overalls. My mother made all my clothes. Flour sack dresses. I had flour sack bloomers.

Was Primary on a Sunday, like it is now?

No. I think it was on a Tuesday. Mutual was on a Tuesday too. When I went to Mutual, it was on a Tuesday. I can remember they had so many parties at the church, and we just partied. They don't do that now. Everyone would bring food, and we would have supper, and I remember they had stairs down in the basement. They would lay boards across them and put their babies on them to sleep while everyone else danced. They had a lot of dances, and they don't do anything anymore. My dad played for the dances.

What did your dad play?

The piano. He chorded.

Did you ever learn to play the piano?

Oh, I took lessons for years, but it didn't take.

Did you learn to cook as a child, or when you got married?

Both. I remember learning to cook a roast from my mother-in-law. I'd never done that before.

Did you grow up with your husband?

He moved to town. I was a freshman and he was a senior. He didn't pay any attention to me. He had lots of girlfriends. I'll have to tell you my first date with him. The war ended, and his service. They let him come back home when it was through. I was working at the drugstore scooping ice cream. He came up to me, and he said, "You still love me?" You know, I was a kid, and I said sure. So, he asked me for a date, and that was it.

What year were you born? What kinds of things were happening in the world as you were growing up?

1926. I don't remember dates and things like that. I remember my birthday, August 5th.

What was your favorite time of year as a kid?

Summer. I don't like winter anymore. I don't know that I ever did. I just know that I like summer, spring, and fall.

Did your family ever go on any trips together?

Not really. We had cows, and we always had to milk the stupid things.

Did you ever get hurt as a child?

No, but my brother was forever getting hurt.

Did your family play a lot of games together? What kinds of games did you play?

Checkers. That was the most. By the time I got old enough, we had Monopoly and lots of games. I played baseball when I was in eighth grade. I wasn't any good. I wasn't good at anything. I wasn't really into sports. I never got to play pitcher; I was always shortstop. I didn't particularly want to play pitcher. I enjoyed it, but I didn't excel in it. I didn't excel in anything.

My Life: Stories and Lessons

When you were a kid, were you barefoot a lot?

All the time! I remember my mother always said, "Now you wash those feet before you go to bed."

What kind of house did you grow up in?

The one on the farm had two bedrooms upstairs, one bedroom downstairs, and no bathroom. No electricity. We had an outhouse. I remember sharing a room with my two brothers and my dad and mother. My dad snored. Glade, my husband, did too.

Did you have any embarrassing stories?

There's one embarrassing thing from my life I remember. Primary was a mile from school, so that made it two and a quarter miles back to my home. But this one time, we were heading home from Primary, and I had to go. There were some boys ahead of us, and finally they went over a hill or something, and right at that moment, I wet my pants. And I had flour sack panties on that my mother made me. And they get thick and heavy when they get wet. I was so embarrassed. I wonder if those girls remember who were with me. The boys didn't see. They would have teased me to death. It was so bad. I wish I had a pair of bloomers, just to show you. I was so embarrassed to have to wear bloomers because we couldn't afford panties. Panties were rare.

Did you have any pets growing up?

We always had one. The nice thing was, we'd go down to the neighbors and watch the rock crushers crushing rocks, and when we'd come back there was the dog and cat, waiting for us. In those days, people would put kittens in a burlap bag and throw them in the

Katie with her brothers Wallace (left) and Howard. Note the outhouse in the background.

river. Oh, my brother, he just thought that was terrible, and I did too. That's just what people would do with their pets. One time we had two dogs, I remember. We had sheep, and so we had dogs. My brothers tried to ride the sheep.

Did you and your siblings ever make a secret hideaway or fort?

I remember making a playhouse down in the raspberries once. I hated those things. We had a big garden on the farm. My mother had everything; we didn't go to the grocery store. Lettuce was one of the things we all loved. I hated helping with the garden, too.

Did you have a lot of chores?

Yes, out in the wood box. We had two stoves and a heater. We had fires, and we had to fill the wood box.

What did you use to keep your food cool?

The ditch. We would put it in buckets, and we had a hole where we put the buckets in the water, so it was cold. It's the only thing we had. Oh, it was cold outside.

Did you walk to school no matter what the weather?

We did until winter. Then they had a school sleigh.

Did you like to draw or color?

No. I'm trying to think. I was never artistic in any way.

Did you listen to music or watch movies in high school?

Friday afternoons they would shut everything down, and we would go and watch a movie. I don't remember my favorites. We would listen to music in the car and record players.

Did you have any favorite records?

Oh, of course. It was Frank Sinatra's time.

Did you like to go see plays and musicals? What kinds?

Well, every year somebody in town would put on a play. I was just a little kid then, so I would just get a little kid part, but my brother was in all of them. He loved it. He just loved being in them. In the high school plays I would get a little dinky part. There were two girls who were the most popular girls in school, and they were in everything. They got the leads in all the plays. One of them ended up marrying my nephew, but she is dead now too.

What's your favorite memory from your childhood?

I know that one. I had the dogs dressed in doll clothes. We took the dogs and put them in the buggies and took them around everywhere. They kept trying to get out, and I wouldn't let them. Finally, I helped them. Poor little mother, she was having her puppies. She didn't want to have someone bothering her.

    We had a dog named Sally, and now we have two Sallys in our family. We had lots of dogs, because of the sheep.

Did you take any animals with you when you moved to town?

We took the cows, and we had the dairy farm. We sold the sheep, and we had the chickens for a while. I don't know how we got rid of them. We ate them, I suppose. We would kill a pig in the winter and eat it all winter. Other times, we would kill a chicken when someone came. I learned to pick a chicken and kill it when I was a kid. It was just part of life.

Young Adulthood

Where did you go to high school?

I loved high school. It was a lot of fun. I went to high school in Ashton, and we didn't date till we were sixteen.

Did you not date because you wanted to or because you weren't supposed to?

Don't worry about that.

So, you didn't start dating until you were sixteen?

No, I didn't date till I was sixteen, and of course I had a little fun now and then. It was never too serious.

Did you date a lot of boys?

Oh, yes.

What kind of dates would you go on?

Well, mostly in those days you would just sit out in the car and neck.

Did you go to movies? Did you have a drive-in?

We had a drive-in too, and we went to them. It was down in Rexburg. We went to a few drive-ins, though, and they had cash night. I believe it was Thursdays, and you got in, and when the first show was over, they had drawings. They would give away so much, like five, ten, and fifteen dollars, maybe, but it was a big deal. We just did what average kids do. We would have picnics and go to dances. They had school dances with a school orchestra, so that was fun.

Were they casual dances or did you take a date?

You didn't take a date. It was just matinee dances, was what we called them. It was always fun because we had the school orchestra and my brother was in that.

Did you like to dance?

I was not a great dancer, but I got by with it.

Did you ever have a prom where you took a date?

Oh, yes.

Do you remember what color your dress was?

Hmm. No. That's funny.

Do you remember who you went with?

Yes. He is dead now. Billy Bowersox.

Did you ever date him?

Yes. He still has descendants up in Drummond area. Oh, but I dated a lot of boys. I'm not sure why. I worked in the drugstore. I didn't get popular until I started working there. I gave them a little ample more on each ice cream cone maybe.

What was your favorite subject in school?

I was not a great student, but probably glee club. Once I got into high school, I was into contests. I sang alto, and the way I became an alto was that my girlfriend, who lived around the corner, was the most beautiful alto you've ever heard. Her name was Louise Biorn. I made sure to stand by her, and I would just sing along with her. And then I learned to sing alto.

What kind of things did you do besides glee in high school?

I liked English, I guess, because we had to read. Hmm, what else did I like? I wasn't a very good student, which was my own darned fault. I liked boys then.

Were you friends with her your whole high school?

Yep. Out of my whole graduating class, there were thirty or something, which isn't very many. But there are only four left that I can count that are still alive. There is Glenda (Hill) and me, we always meet at the cemetery on Memorial Day at the same time to put flowers on our folks' graves. We're so glad to see each other because there are four left, but I can't think of the others right now. You think about that when you get old, about how many kids there are left. We had a reunion a few years ago of the whole high school.

They told us the year and everything and all the kids came. It was great.

Did you ever sneak out of the house?

No. Oh, I was a very nice girl. I didn't do anything bad. I guess I was too scared or something. I was a good LDS girl, and I was into my religion. One time I went with a bunch of kids, and I can't remember how many were in the car. You couldn't get in trouble with the kids we dated because there were always so many kids in the car. I can't remember what my curfew was, but I didn't make it on time. My mother came up to find me, and she didn't drive but she walked, and I felt so bad that I had caused my mother trouble.

Did your parents ever spank you?

My father never did, but my mother did. Swatted my rear end. She would put me over her knee and whack.

Who taught you to drive?

Oh, my brother, because they didn't have any place where we could go to learn how to drive a car. He just said "I think it's time you learn how to drive." He took me out on the road, and he taught me to drive.

How old were you when he taught you?

I guess I was about sixteen. I didn't drive till I had a license.

Did you have tractors on your childhood ranch?

No, we only had horses. Other people had tractors, but they had more money than we had. We had to walk to school all the time.

Did you still walk to school in high school?

Yes, all the way through. I lived in town, so we didn't have any buses.

Did you have a vehicle growing up?

Yes, we had a dairy, so we had the milk truck and a car.

Did they let you use the car often?

Oh, yes. Usually my brother drove, and I would run in and put the milk on the porch.

Did you get in a lot of fights with your siblings in high school?

Of course. I have no idea what about, but probably something silly.

Did you ever get into any fights during high school?

Oh, we feuded, kind of, with some other girls. They were going to come beat us up, but they never did. I don't think I went steady until after I graduated. Louise and I never fought over any boys.

When did you graduate high school?

I graduated in '44. In those days the girls would get married and wouldn't go to college. My family didn't have the money to send me to school. My brothers did, but those days the girls got married.

What is the name of your husband?

Glade Lyon.

When did you meet him?

Well, they moved here (to Ashton). I was in my freshman year. Anyway, they moved here, and his dad worked for the railroad, and I never paid any attention to him, and he never paid any attention to me, because I was just a little snot-nosed kid and he was a high-school boy. He was three years ahead of me. He came home from the war, and so then I married him.

How old were you when you got married?

Twenty.

What did you do between graduating high school and getting married?

I worked at the drugstore.

Were you still living at home with your parents?

Yes.

Did your husband ever go overseas?

Oh yes. Japan and Germany, and I think a few others.

Was that for the war or for traveling?

For the war. This was a bad time in my life between high school and getting married. One of the local kids (Ben Brower) came home on

Glade and Katie cutting their wedding cake.

furlough because his brother had died, so he came home for the funeral. That's when we started dating, and then he came home again on furlough before he went overseas. He was the sweetest thing. I never dated a sweeter boy than him, and he was killed. It was awful. I thought my heart was broken.

Were you ever engaged to him?

Oh yes, I had a ring. I had one from Glade too, though.

Were you nervous to get married?

Yeah. My folks didn't approve of the wedding. They wanted us to get married in the temple, and Glade wasn't interested in the temple. He didn't want anything to do with it. But anyway, we got married. Later, my mother told me that Glade did more for her than her own sons had. He would come and fix things for her. That made me feel awful happy, but he decided somewhere along the way that we needed to go to the temple, so we did.

The Idaho Falls Temple?

Yes. The Rexburg temple hadn't been built.

Did that make you happy that Glade decided to get married in the temple?

Of course it did, but it thrilled me more when my mother said that he had done more things for her than her own boys.

Did Glade have a hard time coming back from the war?

I don't think so. He was engaged to a girl from New York, but then we dated for quite a while, so he said "I'd better break it off." So, he did. You know, I was here and she was there, which makes a difference. I don't think she—they had been away from each other for a while, so I bet she didn't wait. I don't know, but I'm just guessing.

Was it popular for boys to date multiple women at the same time?

Well, not really. Maybe they would date once, but that would be it. If they dated twice, then they were probably going steady.

Did you two have a long engagement?

No. He came home around the first of the year, and we were married in December. He had been home almost a year.

Did you go on many dates with him?

Oh, heck yes.

What was your favorite date with him?

Oh, I don't know. In those days we always had two or three couples with us. We were never alone, because we would get in the car and someone always had to sit on someone's lap. We could never get more than three couples in the car.

Did you get to sit on his lap?

I suppose so. That was so many years ago. I'm 92 now. If I was 20 when I got married, then it was a long time ago.

Did you have different rules in dating than we do now?

Yeah. Girls, we all talked about everybody, because LDS girls had a different rule of life than the other girls did.

How would the men ask girls out on dates?

They would just come up and say, "How about going to a dance with me?" They had the matinee dances, which was fun because you could dance with all the kids. The formal dances were always a little more formal.

Were you ever disappointed that you didn't go to college?

No. I just wanted to get married and to have a home. My brothers went to college.

Was Ricks College built then?

No. Wait a minute. It must have been. Yeah, it was built. My brothers and husband went there. He went to college at Moscow his first year, and then we got married, so he didn't get to finish. He had to run the store because his dad died. That's what he did was work and run the store.

Did you guys decide to have kids right away?

No. I used to cry every Mother's Day because I didn't have any kids. I wanted a family so bad. I remember crying on Mother's Day, but we had been married four years before I finally got pregnant. I had a miscarriage in there too. I wanted a family so bad, and I was so glad when I got one.

Did your husband want kids as bad as you?

Oh, he didn't want any. He told me before we were married. He said he didn't like kids—well, little kids. He wasn't sure he wanted kids at all. We had a cousin, or his cousin had a baby when we did. The baby (Blake Hill) was just a little older than ours, and we went with them to the hospital to bring him home. Many a time I tried to get Glade to hold their baby, but he wouldn't do it. He just wouldn't do it. When Jack was born I was so afraid that he wouldn't have anything to do with him, but when we were ready to go, he just reached out and carried him out. Loved him with all his heart. He was pretty proud of him.

Were you worried that he didn't like kids when you married him?

Not really. I am not sure. It's hard to remember. He never complained when I got pregnant, and he always seemed to be happy.

Did you have any problems with your pregnancies?

No, I had the neatest pregnancy you ever saw. I was never sick. No morning sickness whatsoever. I wasn't sick with any of my kids. I don't even know. I just waited and waited to get sick and I never did.

What kinds of things were important for you to teach your kids?

I taught them not to swear. We always went to church except for my husband, he didn't go to church. The kids and I did, and it was across the street, which was nice. Between sacrament meeting and Sunday school I would go home and put a roast in, so when I got home it was ready to eat. Glade knew I wasn't going to change, and so he decided to take me to the temple, and he came from a very religious family, so it wasn't hard. My kids lived like I did when I was at home. We had blessings and we said the prayers and everything. We participated in all of it, and I had learned that from home. We

Ashton Ward building, across the street from the Lyon home.

(when I was a child) knelt down around the kitchen table chairs and said our prayers.

Did you ever discuss with him why he didn't want to go to church?

Oh, he just got in with a bunch of kids in high school to begin with. I was glad when he straightened out. He smoked when I first got married to him, and my folks frowned on that. When I got pregnant with Jack, then he quit, because there shouldn't be smoke at home with a baby.

How did you discipline your kids?

About the same way as my parents. I swatted them once or twice, but they were never beaten or anything.

What are some things you like to do?

I quilt. That's my life. I taught six girls from the college how to quilt. Two of them came back one day and wanted to quilt, so I helped them. This one girl said, "This is a beautiful quilt," and I said "This isn't beautiful, this is a scrap quilt. If you want to know what a quilt looks like, I'll show you." So, I took her in my room, and I had the quilt on my bed that I made. I think it's an outstanding quilt, because so much work went into it. I have on my wall a picture of my great-grandmother coming across the plains, and she's dying. She's buried at Chimney Rock. It's quite the story, all in itself. I'm very proud; I almost cry when I tell it. So these girls who were looking at the quilt, one was looking at the quilt, and the other was looking at my great-grandmother. And I said, "Are you familiar with that?" And she said, "Oh, yes, my mother has a picture of it in her living room." They were from Alaska! Then I said, "Well, we're cousins," and this girl jumped up and down and grabbed me and loved me, and she said "I love cousins." After that they came back again, and I said, "Well, did you find out if we're related?" She said, "Oh, yes." She said that her mother got out her genealogy and found out we were cousins. It was not through my dad, but it was through one of my dad's brothers or sisters, it was that line. That's how we got to be cousins.

Did you learn to quilt as a child? Did your mother teach you?

My mother always had a quilt, but I didn't. I just sat down and started quilting! It just comes natural. But I didn't quilt until after I was married. I started making quilts. I have a folder in my room that's a picture of each quilt. I've made over a hundred. They're all beautiful, I think. I have four kids, and they've all got kids, and each of them have two or three quilts. I tried to give them one when they got married. They've all got two or three. All of them.

You should see my material room; it looks like a store. My husband built shelves, and I pull out a drawer, and it's just full of material. But ever since he died—he died twelve years ago—I haven't made any quilts. And now I'm too old. Well I haven't really tried it. But like I said, I think quilting was my life.

My mother quilted, and I watched her, so that's how I learned, I guess. It's quite a bit of work putting one of them on the frames. I didn't do that until after I was married. I did it with just doing it. Nobody showed me, I just did it.

Did your mother ever help make the quilts?

No, she didn't. She died before I ever started quilting. But she would have been pleased.

When did you start quilting? Did you have any other hobbies while you were married?

Oh, I could crochet. I crocheted a lot, and I did a lot of embroidery. You were supposed to have a set of dish towels and a couple sets of pillowcases, so I had them all done and stored in my cedar chest.

Did all girls have cedar chests in high school?

Oh yes. You had to have a cedar chest. I mean, not all girls had them, but I remember I paid thirty dollars for mine. You would buy your material and make dish towels and pillowcases. I had a sister-in-law that was fantastic. She could do anything that had to do with handwork.

What kinds of things did you wear in high school?

Oh, my mother didn't make those outfits. I bought them from JC Penny's. We didn't wear jeans at all—mainly dresses, but then they started wearing jeans or slacks a little toward the end. It was about half and half. They sold patterns, and I made a lot of my clothes, and I enjoyed that. I did them on a treadle sewing machine.

Did you make clothes for your kids?

Yeah, sure did. In fact, I made some T-shirts which had the biggest neck that you ever saw. Maybe it was my grandkids that I had made them for. I saw a picture of them in that shirt, and his mother says, "No, it's all right." Just because I had made it, she was going to see that he wore it.

Did you use a sewing machine or do it all by hand?

No, with dresses you use a sewing machine.

Did you make your boy's clothes as well?

I made a lot of T-shirts. No pants. I suppose we bought those.

Did you make any clothes for your husband?

Oh, heavens no. At the store we sold men's clothing too. Some women's, but no, I knew better than to make him any clothes.

So you and your husband owned that store your whole married life?

Yes. It was in town, and we sold the store and retired when he turned 65. That was just pure heaven. We stayed in Ashton, but we

Lyon's Store, about 1968.

were always going on rides to roads we had never been on before. I sure enjoyed that, and I miss that a lot.

What kind of car did you drive?

A Chevrolet. Well, his mother when we got married, and his dad was alive as well, they bought a car, and I can't remember what it was, but they gave us their Pontiac, so we had a car then. We drove it for a long time, and we didn't have any money to buy another one. It was two colors—dark blue on top and creamy or something on the bottom. It was a stick shift.

When you were married did you have any callings?

First, I was in the Primary, and then I was in Mutual, and I didn't like it. We had little kids, and it was just hard to go at night and leave little kids. When it was time to go to Girl's Camp, I had four kids, with Kathy being a baby. We had a little trailer, which was the littlest thing you had ever saw. We all slept in it, and he took the trailer up there with the three girls. Nobody objected, and Kathy was the most popular baby. She was passed around to everybody. She was only about five months old. It was by Jack Young's Ranch.

How long would you guys camp for?

I don't remember. I do remember that we just slept out in the open. We didn't have any tents or sleeping bags. We went up to Cave Falls, up by their campground, and we camped kind of close to the road. We took all our quilts, and we slept under all those quilts. I can't remember if it was warm or cold. The next morning when we got up, there were bear tracks all the way up the road. I am scared to death of bears to this day.

Have you ever come close to one?

Oh, yes. Dumb people. Right after we were married, we didn't have any kids yet, but we went with another couple to Cave Falls or something like that, and there was a bear. We saw a little cub playing by the side of the road, and man it was cute! We got out and started playing with that cub, and down a ways was his mother.

She never came down and never got worried. We were so dumb, and we didn't know anything. It's a wonder she didn't come and do anything. It was a black bear. You couldn't get me out of the car, though. I was scared of bears, and I don't like them.

Did you travel more at the beginning or end of your marriage?

We went on a trip every year of our marriage, or at least we tried to. We took the kids and tried to show them the world or the states. We didn't make it to all of them, but we almost made it to darn near all of them. It was so great. We had potato harvest, and that is when we took the kids and went on vacation.

What was your favorite trip? Is it hard to pick one?

It was really fun to go to Europe and all the countries there and see everything. You take pictures and then put them away and never see them again. But Glade and I went on a trip every year. When we went to Europe we went to Belgium, France, Portugal, England. It was fun. Portugal was my favorite. The people only come to here [showing with her hand how tall they were]. Oh, they were cute people. We went to Mexico a lot. We went with a bunch of people in trailers. We stayed at different places.

Was it weird for your husband to go back to the places he and served in during the war?

No. We went to France, but I don't think so.

Did you ever go swimming in the ocean on your vacations?

We didn't call it swimming, but we went in the ocean. My kids were all good swimmers, but I wasn't.

Were you scared of sharks?

I never thought about it, but after seeing that thing on TV about the sharks about scared me to death. Somewhere I saw sharks. We went one time when school was out for harvest to Disneyland for vacation. We had a ball, and we loved every minute of it. Then the next year we went to Oregon and just parked on the beach with our trailer and just had a ball. The next year, we asked the kids where they wanted to go, and they all said Oregon, so we went to Oregon every year. I loved Oregon. I love Washington too, but I think Oregon was my favorite. We went to Newport, Oregon, every year just because we liked it. We went to Colorado and New York.

Did you drive all the way to New York?

Yes. Not me, but Glade did. There was a lot of yelling, with Glade yelling at the kids to be quiet.

What kinds of things would you give them to distract them?

Oh, we had coloring books and all sorts of things—anything we could think of. We would even buy them new little toys, so they had something new.

I can't see how any of this could be interesting to anybody.

Is there anything you would go back and change about your life now that you are older?

Probably, if I could remember it.

Glade and Katie on the beach. Katie is holding beach agates in her left hand.

Do you feel like life in high school was slower then than it is now?

Well, it was slower, because not every high-school kid had a car like they do now. Anyway, it was lots different, because kids didn't have cars, but we just walked a lot, I guess. I remember a lot of the kids would get their parents' car when we had a dance or a date or something.

Did you ever ride a bike anywhere?

Oh, yes. When war came on, my brother sold me his bike. It was a boy's bike, and he regretted it his whole life. He says, "Why didn't I just give it to you?"

Did your brothers go to war?

Two of them went to war. Howard was such a good kid. He was one of those kids who lived his religion completely. I don't remember what he did when he came out, but my brother Wallace, he went to school on whatever the veterans had. So he got a good college education, including a doctorate degree. They were different than they are now, but anyway, he spent his whole lifetime being a soldier. His kids grew up all over the world.

Both of your brothers survived the war?

Yes. My one boyfriend was the only one who never came home.

Did they have a hard time coming home from war?

Not that I ever knew. Howard had a girlfriend, and they got married when he got home. He had to make a living. She died last year, and my brother died before that.

Do you have one brother who is still alive? Did he go to war?

Yes and yes. He is the one that got the good education and went to college and all that.

Did you cut your hair short while you had kids?

I kept it medium length. I started going to beauty salons, though. It has been a long time since I have washed my own hair.

Adulthood

How did your husband propose to you?

We were coming up the road from St. Anthony to Ashton, and when we got to the Fall River Bridge, he says, "Oh, I never ever proposed to you." We had already set our date to get married. So there was a place you pull over to park. He pulled off to park, and he proposed. I said yes, and we started home, and we got stuck in the snow and couldn't get out. Somebody came and pulled us out.

Did it surprise you when he proposed to you?

Well, I didn't know it was coming, but he hadn't formally. He just thought he'd better take care of that.

Did he get down on one knee?

Oh, no! There was snow everywhere, so he just played it how it was.

Where did you work after high school?

I worked a lot of places. I worked most of our life, in our store, Lyon's store. Before I got married, I was working in the drug store.

Katie in front of the Star Theater, just west of the City Drug Store, on the bicycle she'd bought from her brother Howard. The movie posters in the window date this photo to 1944, the year Katie turned eighteen.

What did you do at the drugstore?

I was just a clerk. I just loved it!

Did you get along with your coworkers?

Yes! I got along fine. In fact, I was there with my niece.

What are some of your best memories working there?

Oh, I don't know. It was just a gathering place of kids, and it was just a happy place. Everybody treated me really nice, and it was just a happy place.

When did you stop working there?

I don't remember. Darn.

After you got engaged, did you continue working?

Oh, yes.

Did you still help out at the store when you started having kids?

Oh, sure. I took them with me. In those days, you kind of drug your kids around with you, because you didn't have babysitters like you'd like to, so you just drug your kids along.

When was the moment you knew you were in love with your husband?

I don't know. I didn't say anything, either. I just didn't think that I should say it first. I thought I would leave it up to him, so I did.

I knew his family was so happy because we were going to get married. He had a girl back in New York, and she wasn't LDS. She was Catholic, in fact, very strong in her beliefs and all. And he was marrying me, LDS faith. It was just what they wanted in a daughter. It made my mother-in-law, I think, like me all the time.

Where and when did you get married?

In my brother's home; he was the bishop. December 1st, 1946. I graduated in 1944.

Where did you go for your honeymoon?

Salt Lake. It was December 1st, and we stayed a week. It was an awful snowstorm. Just terrible. Traffic just couldn't get anywhere, but we just sailed along; we had snow tires. They didn't have snow tires much back then, so we did good. We just sailed along, and we didn't get stuck. We had a picture of us in our car after we were married, and the snow was as high as our car. We didn't take it to show that, it was just in the picture.

What kinds of things did you do on your honeymoon?

Just people things. We went to the movies, ate out, and that's all I remember.

How long was your engagement?

Three months, I think, or something like that. I really can't remember, but neither one of us believe in long engagements.

Did you plan certain things for your wedding?

No. We were just married in the home. My dear sister-in-law, she was a treasure. She kind of handled most everything. Glade's family and my family were big,[3] so to fit in that house and get married, I don't know how we did it.

Did you buy a wedding dress, or make one?

No, I bought one. I made Robin's wedding dress. I can't even remember what the other girls' wedding dresses were like. Only my daughter-in-law. I got a letter from my daughter-in-law the other day, just thanking me for being a good mother-in-law and everything. It was really sweet. I called her my favorite daughter-in-law, so her letter to me was to her favorite mother-in-law.

Did you pick out your wedding ring or did Glade?

I had a gold band. I can't remember why we changed. Oh, it's because we couldn't afford a diamond and it bothered him. Anyway, when he got enough money that he could afford a diamond, he was tickled. It was just because everyone else had one. I told him I didn't care if I had a diamond or not as long as I had a wedding ring. I got both, though. Glade got me this ring on my finger, too. It's opal. He gave me a lot of rings because he couldn't think of anything to buy me, so he bought me jewelry. I got earrings out the ying-yang.[4]

Do you like jewelry?

Yeah, I kind of do.

---

3. "Glade's family" probably included his mother's parents with their children and families.

4. "I love this!" says daughter Suzanne.

Did your husband compliment you a lot?

I don't remember, if that's terrible. I suppose he did.

What was it like being a newlywed?

We didn't have a lot of money. He had a lot of money saved up, and we used all that. I worked, but still it was hard. It was okay, though—just part of living.

What was your first house like?

We lived in a corner home upstairs and rented it. It was a kitchen and room and a bathroom we shared. I didn't like that. The lady was just real nice, but it didn't have a fridge. How do you live without a fridge? And then an apartment became available in the hotel, and we took it. We'd only been in the other house six weeks, or a month, something like that. She was really hurt that we moved. It was sure fun in the hotel. We shared a bathroom with the ones across the hall, but that was okay. I'd known them my whole life, and we were good friends. They didn't have any kids yet, and they'd been married for a while. They were good friends. Everybody was friends. Everyone knew everyone, and they were all just good friends.

After that apartment did you buy your own home?

We built it. We bought a vacant lot across the street from the church, and we built a house. It just made a man of Glade. He and a carpenter built it, and he learned from the carpenter. He learned an awful lot, and he learned that he was a good carpenter, and he loved it. He'd never pounded a nail before, I think, and he just loved it. Then when we added on a couple bedrooms, we had an upstairs, and we built a family room. We had a garage, and all that. But we hired a carpenter and a crew to come do that. Glade learned to be a good carpenter, and he could fix anything. He didn't know he could until we got married.

I said I built that house so I could go to church. And we were a block from the grocery store. And everything was just perfect. The first thing they did was change the wards. They tore down the church. When it was across the street, between Sunday school and church, I'd run home, put the roast in the oven, and when I'd get back from church, the roast was done.

Did you guys live in that house your whole life?

Yes. Never lived in any other house. We're in the process now, where we don't know whether to sell it. Anyway, I probably will never live alone again, so I don't know what to do with the house. My kids say they're going to sell it. You know I really don't want to. My husband built it. I really don't want to sell it. But I can see it's silly to pay taxes on something. We were thinking of renting it, but I guess we're going to sell it. They always say they are going to do work on the house. They go for about two or three hours a day if they can. The house still isn't done and ready to sell, but they want to sell it so we don't have to pay taxes on it.

What did your husband do for a career? Did he ever pursue carpentering?

Well, we had the store. His main aim in life, when we first were married, was he wanted to finish college. He went to the University of Idaho first. College kids didn't have cars in those days, so he rode the train to Moscow. It was a darn long ways. It's kind of up north. After we got married, he really wanted to finish school, so he went to Ricks and finished then. He felt like he hadn't accomplished

Mid-century modern Katie.

anything. He graduated and had a degree, even though he worked in the store. He just felt like he'd missed something. But that's okay, he was his own boss.

Did you have any pets?

I remember a rabbit. We had several dogs. One of them got distemper and died. We also had cats and a mynah bird. Yeah, we had pets.

How long after you got married did you have your first child?

Four years. I used to cry on Mother's Day, because I wanted them. Glade didn't want them when we first married, but when we did have them, he was just crazy about them.

What is the order of your four children?

Jack is about 65, 66. Suzanne is two years younger. Robin is four years younger. Then Kathy is about five years younger. I'd never do that again—have so much time between the kids. They need to be closer to the same age so they can play together.

Did you spread them out on purpose, and why?

Yeah. I don't know why.

Did you give birth in the hospital? Were they long lasting?

Yes, and just normal. I do remember, Glade was in the hospital—I think he had an appointment or something—and a lady came in and had a baby while he was there. You could hear her scream all through the hospital. I was so scared that I would do that. I was just about to give birth, and I worried about that. Glade always reassured me that I would be just fine. I just did fine.

Did it hurt?

Oh, yeah. After he was born, I asked Glade if I yelled, and he said, "No you didn't." I was happy. I wanted to, I'll tell you.

What hospital were they born in?

In the Ashton hospital. We had a really nice doctor. They'd come from far and near just to go to our doctor. Darn him, he loved to fly airplanes. He took his plane up one day and crashed on a mountain and died, so that took care of him. After that, everything just went downhill.

What was it like for you becoming a new mother?

Oh, it was just heaven. I loved that little boy.

Did he make you stay up at night?

Oh, yes! He would eat a bottle. I never did get enough milk to feed him, it just didn't happen. One time, Glade's cousin—she had a baby just about the same age—one day she nursed him. He didn't throw it up! I just about made her come live with us. I tried for three kids, my milk just didn't come in. I'm not sure why. But the last one, I didn't even try. I had a bottle sterilizer. We'd put all the bottles in the sterilizer, then fill them with milk, or formula, and then we'd just keep them in the fridge until I was done. Then we'd do it again.

Did you get along with your in-laws?

Oh, yes! We both lost our fathers, just a few months after we married. They were just a few months apart when they died. It was a hassle really, she was alone. So sad, and she worked in the store, and she just kept right on working. It's just sad to be alone. I don't know how to tell you, but don't ever let your husband die.

Did your two families get together?

No. Well, we lost both our fathers, so I don't know. We just didn't do it in our family. There wasn't many in his family. I had his mother over for dinner every Sunday. First of all, I'd just ask her to come. Finally, I just said, "Oh gosh, I want you to come to dinner, so just come. You're invited, and I don't have to ask you." And so, she did. Glade had a younger sister. She was about twenty when we got married. She could sure play the piano. She still does. She says she can't go into a church, or they say, "Hey, our organist is gone today; can you play?" They say that to my son, too. He can play without music and sit down and play. It's nice. He can play by ear pretty well, but we gave him lessons with the best piano teacher. He loved it; he still does.

Did you put all your kids in piano lessons?

Yes. I think they all learned to play a bit.

Were there certain hopes you had for your children?

I suppose. Jack wanted to go to college; he did. When Suzanne came along, she wanted to go to college. They and Kathy all majored in English. Jack ended up an author. He's written several books—including Church books. He was named after his grandfather, Glade's father. They were so tickled when we got married.

Did you get into a lot of fights with your husband? If you did, how did you get over it?

No. We just kind of both got mad, and that was it. We didn't really fight much.

Did you and your husband have lots of deep conversations?

Yeah. I loved going down to Salt Lake, because then we talked all the way down and back, and we went once a month. We had to buy stuff for the store.

Did you take the kids with you?

No. My mother watched them.

Did you visit a lot of temples when you were married?

Well we weren't married in the temple, but we went to the temple. Jack and Suzanne were both born, and so was Robin. We went with Kathy in street clothes, when she was a baby, and they had to change her clothes to be sealed. Suzanne was so proud, because she dressed her and undressed her.

What was the feeling like when you got sealed?

I was really happy. He went to the temple because I wanted to, but that was all right. He smoked when we got married, and when Jack was born, he quit. He didn't even tell me. I guess he was waiting for me to notice. Then finally he told me.

Beautiful even without makeup.

Did your kids like sports?

They were not athletic kids. Jack didn't play football or anything like that. Suzanne was on the drill team. I played baseball.

Did they like to sing?

Oh, yes. They harmonized beautifully—Jack especially, he harmonizes. Oh, and Suzanne, she's so good. I don't think Robin would let you hear her sing. Kathy's a great little singer too. Just in cars when we went on vacation, we sang everything we could think of.

Were your kids named after anyone?

Jack was named after Glade's dad. Suzanne wasn't named after anyone, but Susan was the most popular at that time. We didn't want another Susan, but we liked the name of Susan, so we named her Suzanne. Robin is a family name—Glade's mother's family, their name was Robins. Kathy just was because we liked the name. We didn't want another Katie. We've got a Katie, and a Katie, and a Kate, and a Kathy.

Was anyone in your family named after your father?

Yes, my great-grandson Brigham. You should see him. He's the cutest thing you ever saw. He's still a baby. Well, he can crawl.

Were all your kids well behaved?

Oh, yes! They were perfect kids. They weren't bad kids. They really weren't bad kids. In fact, Jack and his friend, they talked about all the bad things they did when they were in high school, and I didn't know about them. I just thought they were the best kids in the world. I don't know if it was that bad.

What was the hardest thing for you about being a mother?

I don't think it was hard. I think it just came naturally. I don't think it was hard.

What was your favorite thing about being a mother?

Just having a home, an income, and kids. It was just a natural thing, that's all.

Did you teach your kids how to quilt?

I don't really remember teaching them how to quilt, but they all do. They grew up with a quilt in the house every day, and they watched me. I watched my mother, and that's kind of how I learned to do it.

What's something that you've learned from your kids?

Maybe patience. I remember when they were sick, how I was afraid they were going to die. I think I was a good mother. I know a lot of mothers are. We had lots of friends, and their kids were all the same age. The kids enjoyed it.

When did you decide you were going to go on family vacations together?

When our kids got old enough that they could enjoy them too.

Did you ever leave some of the kids home?

When we went on vacation we always took all the kids. We went to Oregon all the time for vacation. We actually made it coast to coast on vacations.

Were your kids good travelers?

No. Yeah, they were pretty good. They were normally ready to go. They weren't bad. Of course, there's the usual spats and fights. "You're taking up too much room," you know.

What was their favorite vacation?

Probably Oregon. Of course, we took them everywhere else, too. They loved going to Disneyland and places like that.

Have you ridden in an airplane a lot?

Yes, when we went to Europe. I wasn't nervous. I had been up before we went to Europe.

Did you ever go on a cruise, or anywhere in a boat?

Not any cruises. We went on a tour, that's when we went to Europe. Glade sold more TVs than anyone, so we won a trip to Europe. He had to pay for me to go.

Did you like the food when you visited other countries?

I do remember we went to one country, and I can't remember, but it might have been Mexico. They served us and there wasn't any bread. I said to Glade that I came to see what all the breads were like in these countries. So, when the waitress came by I told her she forgot the bread, and she looked a little funny, but she brought a little bread. It was just plain old baker's bread. In some places, I guess most every place, they told us not to eat off the street. And so we didn't. It was probably perfectly all right, but we didn't. Let's see, I think it was Mexico, and I can't remember what I wanted to eat so badly, but before we got on the plane to go home, I ate off the street. I felt just fine. It might have killed me, but I am still here.

Was it hard to get older for you and Glade?

I don't think we ever thought about that. We didn't worry about that at all. I worried about it; I didn't want to be left alone. I was left alone, and it's been twelve years—a long time to live alone. I guess that's why I'm so happy here, because I don't have to do anything. My meals are ready and on time, and I'm gaining weight.

I've had some bad luck, though. I've lost two teeth, one here and one back there. It makes me mad to be chewing on something and then have it hurt. I don't know how to have them taken care of. They both broke off. When you're 91 years old, you don't feel like putting a lot of money in your mouth, so I don't know what to do. I need Glade here so badly to tell me what to do. We must've talked, because I miss talking to him. I really miss him when I need somebody to talk to. He was a lot smarter than I was. He kept telling me I was just as smart as he was, but he's full of bologna. I didn't want to go to college, I just wanted to get married.

Did you have a lot of gatherings at your house?

Yes. I remember that I put on a dinner party, and it was when our house was little. It was before we had the add-on. I can remember having a table set up in the living room, because we didn't have a dining room then. I just remember having this dinner and inviting

Katie and Glade at Robin's house, March 27, 2004.

people. But I invited a couple who we kind of knew in town. They were in business too.

Did you go stay with your kids when they had a new baby?

I did with Jack. I guess I did with Suzanne, too. They were all here in Ashton. I didn't go to live with them, they came home. All of them.

Did all your kids marry locals?

No. Jack married a girl from Ohio. He met her at BYU. They live in Salt Lake. Oh, she's a delight with her talents.

Suzanne married Larry. I can't remember where he came from.

That's terrible, to not remember where your daughter's husband comes from.

Robin married Rodolfo Rivas, who came from Mexico.

And Kathy's husband came from Oregon.

Do you love having grandkids?

Yes! Yes! We just had a new one, I haven't even seen him yet. He was just born last week. I have twenty grandchildren, and one of them is married, so I hope someday they'll give us a another great-grandchild. I don't know, they're both in college, and it's hard.

Do all of your grandchildren live in Eastern Idaho?

No, I wish they did. Katie, she lives about three blocks from here. She's got five, and gosh they're the cutest kids. I think the more they grow, the cuter they are.

Life Lessons, Family Heritage, and Other Topics

What brought you to the Homestead?

The reason that I'm here is I fall down too much. And believe me, it hurt me. I've got a therapist that I'm working with now. I've got a walker, so I don't fall down so much. I have a bruise that's still healing. It's on my leg. I'd show you the bruise, but I don't think I should. It's this wide, and it's purple and black. It goes clear down here past my knee, that's how hard I fell. I couldn't get up. My knees, they're worn out. I've had both hips operated on, so I can't pull myself up. But I have a thing [a medical alert necklace]. As soon as I call, they dispatch. And with my room right there, it makes it easier. Did you know they have church right here? It's just really nice. And the beauty shop is right there. I'm getting a perm next week.

Do you have a best friend here at the Homestead?

Yeah, she sits at the table to eat with us. There are four of us. I don't know how old she is. She's probably in her sixties or seventies, but we're really good friends. I love being here and being taken care of, but there is one lady here, every week she looks a little different because she is aging. I feel so bad because I can see her going downhill. She always has a smile for you. That's what I want to remember when I am dying is to keep on smiling. I want to be happy and not complain.

A new woman moved here to the Homestead because her husband had died. I asked her what her name was, and she said it was Murdene. I knew a lady with that name from back when, and I knew she was at this dinner party I had given. I asked her if she'd ever been to my house for a dinner party, and she says, "Oh, no, I don't remember." I said, "I think you were there." She had been to my house before. In fact, we were really good friends. Well, she's moved here now, and we've become friends again. She sits at our table to eat.

Who made your quilt frame?

My husband, Glade, made it. The thing I miss the most about him, though, is talking. I just I need someone to talk to all the time, and he was it.

Did he talk a lot with you?

He was very well educated. He would never sing unless we were in the car. The family would sing in the car, and so he would sing with us. He could sing just fine, but he didn't like people to hear him sing.

Did he sing in the shower?

Nope, I never heard him sing in the shower, but I would have liked to have.

Did you guys ever sing together?

I don't really remember. I am sure we did in the car.

What kinds of things did Glade build for you or fix for you?

He built the house, but he had a carpenter to guide him through that. Oh, he just fixed anything. I can't really think of anything else.

He built your quilt frame and shelves for your craft room, right?

Oh, yes.

Did he ever have to make you more than one quilt frame, or did it last for while?

No, he just made the one. I had baby quilt frames and the big one.

What was his favorite thing to build?

I don't know. He was always building something with the kids.

Did they ever build a treehouse?

They had one that Glade built, also a playhouse.

Have you always worn glasses?

I didn't wear glasses until I was a senior in high school, and then I only wore them when I wanted to. When I got married I was in glasses again, and I still am.

Did Glade wear glasses too?

Yeah, he wore glasses. He wore them when I first dated him.

Did your kids all need glasses too?

Let's see. Suzanne was the first of my kids that had to wear glasses and was in the second grade and has worn them ever since.

Have we ever asked you your favorite color?

I think you did. I think it was blue. Maybe.

How many boys did you have again?

Just the one boy. I have a great-grandson now, Sam, and he is the only boy in their family as well. It is kind of interesting, because he is so much like Jack. He likes to be alone and to study. He is so smart.

How old is your grandson?

I think he is in the seventh or eighth grade. We have only got one boy [John] who has a son who can carry on the family name. He just had a baby [Jude] like two weeks ago. He told me he wouldn't be

a good father, and he didn't want to have kids. Now he just worships them.

Did you notice a lot of you and your husband's traits in your kids?

Oh, not really. Except that they pretty much inherited Glade's brains. They were all straight-A students.

Do any of your kids like to quilt as much as you do?

They all know how. Suzanne likes to quilt.

Do any of them use the more modern quilting machines?

I had a friend, and she would come and quilt with me all the time. Her brother bought a quilting machine, and then he went into business with it and quilted for people. So she didn't make quilts anymore, which made me sad, because I enjoyed quilting with her. She retired very young.

Did you ever sell your quilts?

No. I gave them all away.

Which quilt is your favorite?

I don't know. I have a picture of each one of them. There are two or three of them that look alike, with the same color and everything. The one I have on my bed could have been one of my favorite ones. I liked them all.

Did you make any of your quilts with different material? Like T-shirts or ties?

No. I didn't like making them out of T-shirts. That's not good material. Neither are ties. I did use my girl's dresses. They never wore anything out, but I just used the skirts. I used them for scraps.

Is that one of your favorite memories of your mom, when she used to cook?

Yeah. She was always cooking. I enjoyed her cooking. I never really learned to cook until I was married. I remember watching my mother-in-law cook a roast, and I had never cooked a roast. She thought I was able to cook anything, but I wasn't, but I learned quick. Glade never cooked, but at the last he didn't really want to eat much. So he said "I will cook my own dinner," and it was always a can of tomato soup.

Did he eat anything else with it, or just the soup?

Oh, yeah, a grilled-cheese sandwich.

Do you have a favorite thing to cook or eat?

No. I once said hamburgers was my favorite food, and we would cook them out on the deck. But that was just because it was easy, and I could do it easy. It wasn't necessarily my favorite.

Did your kids have a favorite meal they each liked to eat?

Oh, they got to pick what they wanted for their birthday. That got interesting. I don't remember anything right now, but I know we really prepared for it.

Did you have a favorite dessert?

I don't know, but they sure make some beautiful ones now.

As you have grown older, what kinds of things have changed?

Not that I liked them or not, but the hairstyles. They are terrible now. When I was young, a girl had her hair done all the time. I learned to fix my own hair. I just think they are terrible now. We have one girl here, and she washes her hair and just lets it go. A lot of kids do that, though. I don't know why they can't comb their hair.

What things have become important for you? Have they changed from when you were young?

I think my religion, more probably. It means a lot to me. I suppose that's it.

Have you felt closer to God as you have gotten older?

Well, I think so. I sure wear him out sometimes with my prayers, so I must have.

What's some of the most important life lessons you have learned?

Umm, I don't know. All of them, I guess. You just learn as you go.

If you were giving advice to someone on life, then what would you tell them to do?

I don't know what I would tell them. I would tell them to get a job, a steady job, and to support their family. I worry about people that don't work.

Do you have any regrets?

No. I don't think so. I wish I could remember every bit of my life. As you get older, it just gradually disappears. I can't remember nothing, and it makes me so mad. Names and people and everything are hard to remember.

Was it harder to get older for you?

I don't know if it's been harder. It's just a part of God's plan. Something just comes up that you have to do and so you do it. When I was a kid, I was the laziest kid in the world. I didn't like to do anything. I made it.

Did becoming a mother make you less lazy?

Well I don't know. I just think once you get married you are hooked with all that work.

Do you have any favorite memories of your kids or your grandkids?

Oh, yes. I don't remember them, of course.

Has it been hard to watch your friends and family pass away?

Oh, yeah. We buried eight out of the ten children in my family. Of course, it was awful when I had to bury my husband. I heard something in the middle of the night, and I don't know why I was awake. Maybe I was worried about Glade. But I heard something fall, and I thought he dropped something. I sat there and kept thinking about it and worried that it was him, so I went to go check. I saw him on the floor, so I immediately called my girls, and they were there in two minutes. We spent the whole night afterwards talking. I really quite enjoyed the minutes we had together

Do you have a favorite hobby now?

Quilting was all I ever liked. I did really like to cook, too. We cut out every recipe that looked good, and I tried to cook them. I collected lots of recipes. I walked nearly all my life. My friends and I walked, when we were married. There was a bunch of us. Every night at like 5 o'clock. We walked like two miles. I'm still walking. I was walking with one of the therapists the other day, and my shoes, well the sole, was dragging and hitting the floor everywhere I went, so I kicked off my shoes, and I've been in socks ever since.

Did you ever like to play games?

Oh, yes. When I was a kid I loved to play games. When I was a kid we didn't have the games, of course, we didn't even have electricity when I was born. Checkers, that was probably the first game I learned. Nobody would play me. My dad would play with me, but he would always beat me. We played every game that would come along, and after we were married and had the store we actually sold them. We would then take it home and play it. We liked playing cards.

It was so funny. When we retired, he said, "Now I'm planning on going and playing cards with the boys." He went up the first night, and he came home, and he said, "Well, I'm not going to do that anymore." He wanted to go play cards with the guys, but he just said it was boring. He was good to fix anything around the house. Thank goodness.

I have shelves of games and jigsaw puzzles. We had one out here on the table for ages, and it was really weird and hard. I was about to scoop it in the box and bring it in. Someone would go to it and put a couple pieces on every time. I got it in my head I would put in two or three pieces a day too, but I didn't. We finally finished it the other day. One woman got really attached to it and said that she was going home for the weekend and asked if she could borrow it for her family. I told her she sure could, so she scooped it up and took it home. I don't know how she made out.

Do your grandkids ever come and play games with you?

No. Grandpa [Glade] would have played with them forever. He loved games of all kinds and played them all the time.

So how long have you been collecting lions?

Since I got married, and we were married in '46. It was our name, and you would just not believe how many lions we have.

Did you have a favorite?

No.

Did Glade like to go shooting?

We sure did. I could shoot the head off of a pine hen, but I only did it once. I got lots of practice. We went shooting all the time because he loved it. I had really sharp eyes, so I got to go hunting all the time with him because I could sight them and he couldn't. We hunted all the time, and I had my own license. We would go hunting in the fall, and I loved it. I just loved to go hunting with him.

Did you guys teach your kids how to shoot?

Glade did.

Did you guys ever eat what you shot?

Oh, yeah, we ate them all.

Did you hunt deer or elk?

I didn't, but Glade did. He always got his deer, but he didn't always get his elk.

Did he ever use a bow and arrow?

He was very good at the bow and arrow. We lived at the base of the mountains in Ashton, so we had to go hunting, but he loved to use the bow and arrow. He was very good with it. He was good at everything. I couldn't shoot the bow and arrow worth a darn. I considered them men's things. I did hunt, but I never actually got or killed anything. Now I couldn't shoot or kill anything. It would just be horrible. Mother would kill the chickens when we were kids. She would take them to the block and just cut their heads off. I would just stand and watch her, and it would still kick and run without a head for a while. I would go and stop it until it quit kicking.

You have some bowling pins. Do you like to bowl?

Yes. The one on the left is my high bowling score, and the one on the right is Glade's. Glade was a really good bowler and was one of the high scorers on the team. He was on two teams, and I was on two teams. He was on a men's and a pair while I was on a women's and a pair. While the one played then the other would stay home and look after the kids. I really liked to bowl, though.

When did you start bowling?

After I got married. We had little kids, and so we would take turns taking care of them. I am not a very good person to teach anybody anything. I tried to teach my kids how to bowl, but it was disastrous.

Was it exciting for you guys to get electricity in the house?

Oh, yes. We were on top of the world—when you don't have water or electricity and then you suddenly get it. We got it when we moved into town, because they didn't have it in the country.

What was the first appliance that you got?

It was a fridge. You know, my fridge here is so small. One of my little relatives asked me why I had such a tiny white fridge. All that's in it is pop.

Do you like pop?

I usually drink Diet Coke, but I mostly have pop for the grandkids.

What is your favorite snack/treat?

Probably crackers. Club House mini crackers. They aren't as high in calories. When I got diabetes I quit eating all sweets, and I never started again.

So, you got diabetes?

I did get diabetes, and I lost 70 pounds. After I lost 70 pounds though, it just went away.

Did you need to take medication for it?

Oh, yes. I must not have had it very bad to have it go away. But if I gain weight and be heavy like I was, then it will come back.

Did any of your family members ever get sick?

Yeah. I keep thinking about my dad. My dad had rheumatic fever, and he was in bed for months. The doctor would drive his car out there to see him on the farm. If it was winter and the roads weren't open, then he would ride his horse. Now that's a doctor! He also delivered me. I don't think he delivered my mother's first one, because they went to someone out by St. Anthony. After that she had them all at home. Everybody did then, unless you were rich and went to a hospital, but we didn't. I don't think I could do it from home. I am a boob. I wanted to make sure a doctor was there. Even though the doctor wasn't there till the baby came, you at least had the nurses. My brother actually married a nurse, so a lot of my relatives went and became nurses because of her. Then she died of appendicitis. She was a sweetheart and left a whole bunch of little kids for my brother to raise, and he did.

Did you ever get into any accidents?

I might have been in some minor ones. I can't remember if I was a freshman or a sophomore, but we were having our class picnic in the spring, and a car in front of us had a wreck right in front of us. They went around a corner, and we hadn't gone around the corner yet, but when we got there, their car was there upside down. The kids weren't hurt though, and I was surprised. It was a sad class reunion, or whatever it was. Kids at whatever age, when they say they want to drive, I don't care whose kid it is, they just drive you nuts. When they first learn to drive, it is like taking your life in your hands, and I went through it. When I first learned to drive, my brother taught me, and it was lots different. He just took me out on a country road and taught me. I made out all right, though, and didn't have any wrecks.

Did you ever feel like you saw miracles in your life?

I can remember saying that in my life, but I don't remember what it was.

Is there something you wish you could do before you die?

I always liked to cook. Just to have the family to dinner would be just wonderful. I would like that. I don't want to cook a big meal though anymore.

Do you still have family gatherings?

Out on Fall River about four miles, we own an acre, or even a little more. The Point. Glade and I planted every tree out there, and it is full of trees. We carried water to them and watered them and all, and then he finally said, "The creek is right there," so he finally got an irrigation system. We got to water the whole thing then, and then grass came. I could dig sagebrush with the best of you, because it was just covered in sagebrush, and we dug it all out. It has the worst root system.

We sure love the Point, and everybody that wants to and is related will go up there. Glade was going to put a stop to it because people who weren't relatives were going up there and camping. Finally, Glade put a rule on it and said only relatives could stay down there. Now Glade isn't there to see that they do what he wants to them to do. Now one of my girls is in charge of the Point, and so if they call me up and ask if they can stay at the Point, I tell them to call Suzanne. She can tell them quicker than I can. We still let people camp there. There were only chokecherry trees and scrub trees that grow along the river, and then we planted the rest. There is a big ponderosa that a friend of ours planted. It's just enormous—so big and tall.

Did you plant a lot of different trees types?

Mostly quaking aspen and pine.

What do you want your kids to remember about you when you pass away?

That I loved them. I want them to remember. I do love my kids tremendously, and I want them to remember that. My daughter came with her grandson yesterday, and he ran up to me and yelled, "Grandma Great!" He's only four, but I think it's cute that he calls me Grandma Great. I never knew my grandparents, you know, but it is so fun to be a grandmother and a great-grandmother. Maybe I will live long enough to be a great-great, but I only have one married grandchild. She has been married long enough to have a baby now. They were my first great-grandbabies, and they were twins. We said something to the mom about how hard it was to take care of them, and she said she didn't know it was hard. She said she just took care of them, and that is what a lot of people do. They just do what they have to do.

Fashion Show

Fashion Show

Katie showing off what is probably a new coat.

Katie kept this grass skirt in her cedar chest for the rest of her life.

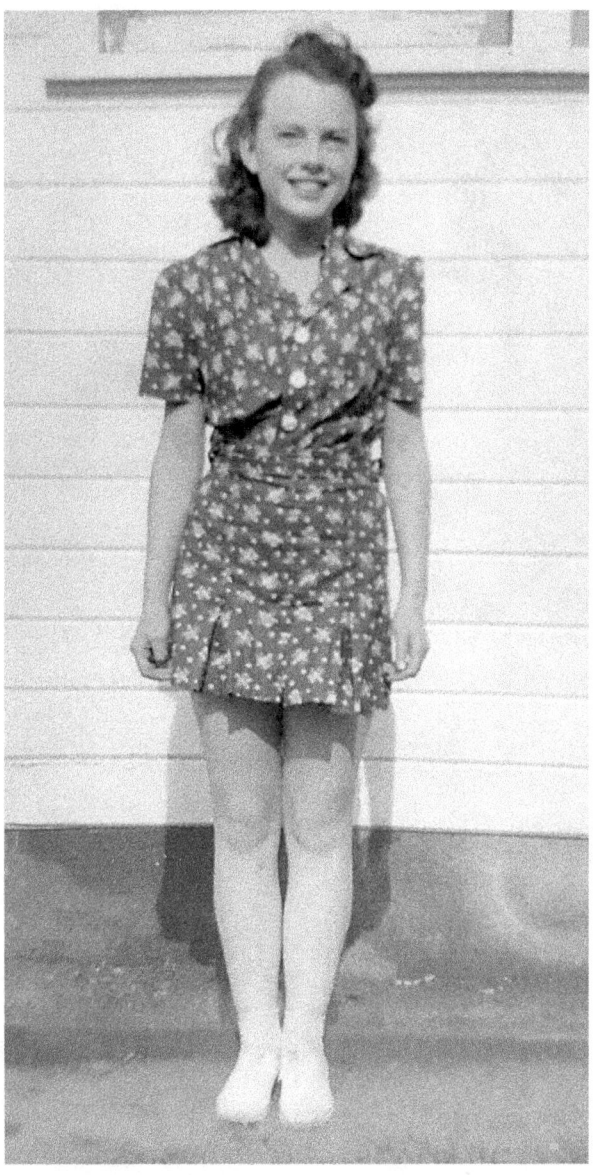

Short!

Standing on the east side of the Murdoch family home, Katie is wearing a formal dress, probably for prom.

This is the same dress (here covered with an apron) that Katie is wearing in the photo on page 52.

Fashion Show

Wearing a fancy dress, Katie is standing on the east side of the Murdoch family home. The house across the street, with the slippery-slide in the front yard, is the home of her brother Tom and his family.

Interview with Leah Anderson, Granddaughter

March 24, 2007

Birth: August 5, 1926. Born to Brigham and Martha Louann (Hammon) Murdoch in Farnum, Idaho, the youngest of ten children.

Land: Brigham and his brother Tom rode horses up here from Utah and homesteaded. When he saw the flat below the Farnum house, Brigham said it was "the most beautiful place in the world." And he knew it was *his*. Now we see moose and deer all the time out there, but back then, they didn't. Once there was a lynx watching Katie's sister Blanche play outside. Brigham killed it.

Activities: Swam in the canal and creek, rode horses, and herded cows. "I was scared to death to ride alone!"

Toys: Dolls, doll bed, cupboard, dishes, no stuffed animals. The family had a radio, and they would listen to *Orphan Annie* and *Jack Armstrong, the All American Boy*. The family seldom went to a movie because it cost ten cents a kid.

Pets: Bum lambs, and dogs—Fritz, Bob, Sally, Jerry. Once she dressed her cat in doll clothes and was trying to put her in the doll

Flat on Fall River.

buggy, but she kept jumping out. Finally Katie realized the cat was having kittens!

School: Farnum Schoolhouse, a mile and a quarter from her house. She was kept out of first grade because her father was sick, so she completed that grade a year later, and then started second grade but switched to third. There were three in her class.

Church: Turned left from the schoolhouse. She now has the rock from above the door at the Point: "Farnum Ward 1909." Her dad, Brigham, helped build the church. All the entertainment was at the church—dances. Brigham played piano, his brother Tom played violin. They rode all over the place to play for dances. Once when Katie and her sister were walking home from church at night, they heard the most awful noise, and they ran to the side of the road

Interview with Leah Anderson, Granddaughter

Rock from above the door of the Farnum Ward building. The inscription says "19 09 Farnum Ward LDS." The rock now marks the entrance to the Point.

and hid. Katie was scared to death! It turned out to be a herd of donkeys coming down the road.

Moved to Town: Brigham got rheumatic fever and nearly died when Katie was six years old. He wasn't able to farm anymore, so they moved to Ashton and ran a dairy. In their new house they had electricity and a bathroom—it was "the most wonderful thing."

Cars: Their family had cars by the time they moved to town. There was no drivers' ed then, so her brother Howard took her out in the country and taught her to drive. Before that, they had horses and a buggy or sleigh. At the church there were all these places to tie up horses.

Brigham and Luanne in front of their home in Ashton.

Activities: Played hopscotch and jumped rope, played baseball and "fox and geese." Still went swimming in the canal, or went to the North Eleven and paid ten cents to swim in the hot springs pool. (Later Grandpa Glade and Grandma Katie bought the North Eleven. It had recently been sold when this interview was conducted, in 2007.) She went ice skating and roller skated a lot, in the (now) "Old" Opera House in Ashton. Once she fell down and broke her tailbone, and after it healed, she was skating again, and as she made her way toward her older sister Tress, she fell down and broke it again! Her family camped a lot, mostly down by Warm River. That's where they would light fireworks on the Fourth of July. "We always had our own firecrackers, all sizes."

Music—Her whole family sang together. They would sing around the piano. Katie got her own piano (which my family inherited!) when she was eleven. It cost around $750. She took lots of lessons and learned to play, but she never felt like she was good enough to play for people.

Jobs—Babysat, delivered milk. She picked spuds, following behind the digger with a basket and sacks. Her very favorite job was working at the Ashton City Drug. She sold everything: liquor, bus tickets, water bills. "Did you make milkshakes?" "Honey, we invented them. People came from miles to get them, and they still do." For taking water bills, her payment was free movie tickets, so she got to go to a lot of movies.

High School—In town there were about thirty in her class. Freshman initiation: go down a big line and everybody would paddle you. You had to bring your own paddle, and then everyone signed it. (She still has hers!) She wasn't involved in student government or sports, but she did public speaking. She was in the glee club for all four years, and she sang alto. They went to competi-

Katie in front of the City Drug Store in 1944. Note the wartime poster behind her in the window. The beautiful dress is the same one she's wearing in the photo on page 52.

tions, and once went clear to Ogden! At dances, her older brother Wallace played trumpet in the school orchestra.

Racism—There wasn't any, because they never saw any other races. The first little black girl she ever saw was at a ward reunion. Katie's brother Tom was against his daughter Tamra marrying Sam, a big black man from Fiji, but she did it anyway, and of course the family came to love him.

Handicapped People—There was one guy who was retarded. He started school but couldn't finish. He married a retarded girl, and they had two kids. Now he rides his bike every day to the post office. Aunt Reha was kind of handicapped—when she was really little, she was out in the Alfalfa field, and her brother didn't see her and he ran her over and cut off her leg!

War—Some food was rationed. They were given meat stamps. Pineapple (and other imported produce) was worth so many points that no one got them. Gas was rationed. "War was not fun." "No boys to dance with; they were all at war."

Dating Life—She dated a lot, but not until she was sixteen. The boys were mostly younger because all the ones her age went to war. They would go to movies (that was "the only entertainment we had"), or on picnics, or for rides. She was engaged to Ben, who was "the most perfect gentlemen." But he was killed in the war (in 1945?). She kept his ring, and after she married my Grandpa Glade Lyon—he had been engaged before too—they used both the diamonds plus an opal he had gotten in Japan to make a ring, which she still has.

Glade Lyon—As a soldier in Japan, he couldn't bring money home, so he bought all the things he could over there—opals, pearls, and diamonds. He had a pet monkey! He was an "aggressive gambler" over there, but he changed when he came back to Ashton.

Married—She married Glade Marvin Lyon on December 1, 1946. They went to high school together; she was a freshman when he was a senior, but had never dated until that year. They dated from February to December, and then got married because "it was too cold to sit out in the car and neck." Her parents didn't want her to marry him, but later, her mother said, "He's better to me than my own sons." Katie and Glade's fathers both died that year, six weeks apart. They lived with his parents, then moved to the Ashton Hotel, then bought a basement house one year after they were married. They then remodeled it into a full three-story house. Glade "was not a carpenter, but he was when he got through."

Jack M. Lyon was born in June 1951 in the hospital in Ashton, which Glade had helped build; he raised a lot of money for it. All of Katie's kids were easy births. Jack was a musical genius—he played the piano, was in the dance orchestra and band. He played by ear (and now he plays a lot more instruments than that!). He also loved to do magic tricks.

Suzanne was born July 1953. She worked a lot and always had a job.

Robin was born April 1957. She was married at age sixteen.

Kathy (my mother) was born October 3, 1961. She was a "good little girl"; no trouble.

All of Katie's kids participated in everything at school, except sports.

Sealed in the Temple—Idaho Falls temple, probably spring 1962. Suzanne changed Kathy into her temple clothes so she could be sealed to the family. Glade and Katie got sealed because a friend said, "We went you to take the temple prep class." So they did! Some friends—Ruth Blackburn and Jean Hammond—took it with their husbands at the same time.

Church—First calling was the secretary of Sunday School. She also taught Primary, Mutual, and Sunday School. She was in the Primary presidency. She got called to serve in the Mutual presi-

Katie on a picnic.

dency, but Glade didn't want her to, so she didn't. She was later in the Relief Society presidency.

Pets—After she got married, they had lots of dogs. They had a mynah bird. It talked, and it was named A.C. Mynah, after Glade's grandpa, Andrew Clinton "A.C." Miner. It would say, "Good morning, Jack."

Vacations—She and Glade and the family would go on vacations every summer. They went to Canada, Disneyland, Massachusetts to visit Glade's sister Connie and her husband Ralph. After Glade retired, they would go to Arizona for the winters; or they went to Mexico, in a trailer or by airplane. Glade spoke some Spanish.

Lyon's Store—It belonged to Glade's parents, and then he and Katie ran it. It was on Main Street in Ashton (where Mountain Mercantile is now). They had it for forty-five years. Downstairs was "Toyland," and Katie ran that. Grandpa was very charitable. One example is Chris Wells, who had all these little kids and no money for Christmas, and Glade gave him credit to buy what he wanted and then tore up the bill. When the store closed he forgave lots of peoples' debts. Grandpa Glade "had his hand in everything"—the movie theater, the Orange Mart in St. Anthony, Potpourri property outside of town (the last of that had just been sold when this interview was conducted). Glade learned Spanish so he could speak to the Mexican customers.

The Point—They bought it when Robin was four. Uncle Tom (Katie's brother) owned all that land down by the river, and he sold Glade and Katie the Point. They would always have Sunday picnics out there with Tom and Alta. Tom would cook hotcakes for all the little kids, in the shapes of cats and dogs. They loved that.

Thanksgiving—One year they had it out in Uncle Tom's cabin, before it was finished. Their table was the door laid over two sawhorses, and they hung a quilt in the doorway to keep out the cold.

Hobbies—Reading library books, started quilting after she was married, she embroidered for her hope chest (before she was married), she learned to tat but didn't do it much, and she learned to knit but didn't do it much—once she knit a sweater for her mom, but she gave it back, so Katie wore it for a long time and then took it to the flea market, and one of her friends bought it and wore it for a long time! Glade and Katie loved to bowl. She belonged to two bowling teams—one for couples (with Glade), and Lyon's team for girls. Another hobby was walking. She and Jean Hammond used to walk two miles every day. She would go clear to Suzanne's house and back in the summer, and would walk laps around the stake center in the winter.

Cooking—She learned most of her cooking in home-ec in school! She didn't know how to cook when she got married. Living with Grandma Lyon was good, she helped Katie a lot. Her first pie was horrible, but Glade ate it anyway. Her favorite thing to cook became anything with bread dough. She got asked all the time to make rolls for funerals. Glade's mom made beautiful rolls, and Katie's mom made biscuits. They were different. Grandma Miner (Glade's grandma, Mette Ann Robins) never went to church because it was her job to cook Sunday dinner.

Journal—She didn't keep one as a kid, but for the last fifteen years she has. Grandpa did too.

Katie on May 15, 2017.

Ethnicity Estimate from Ancestry DNA

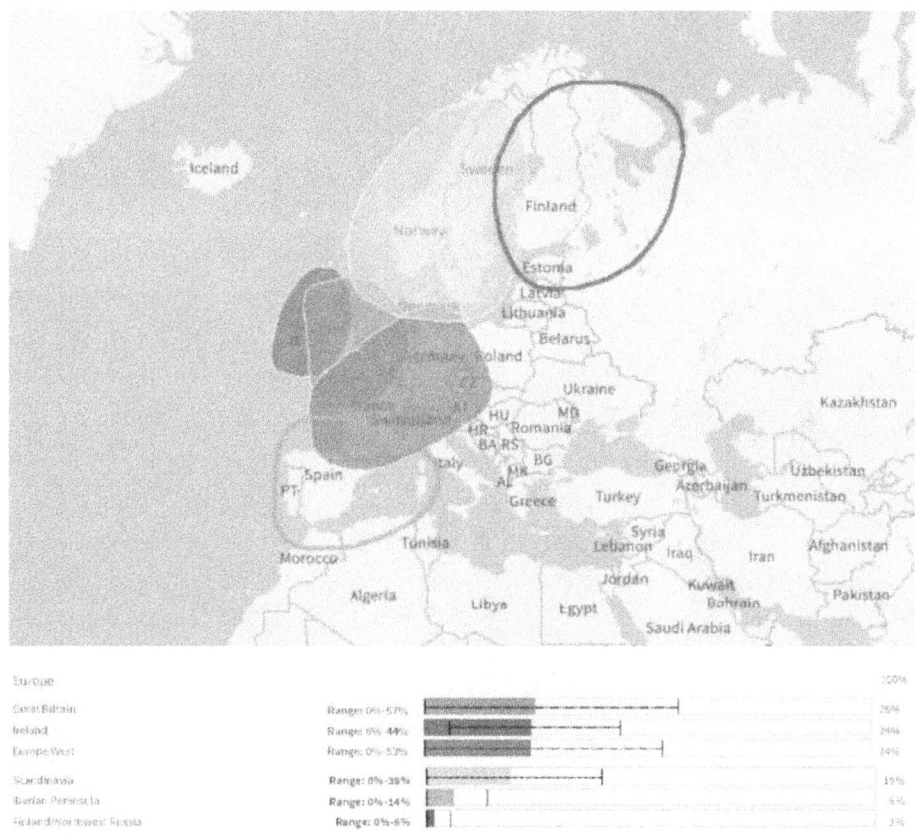

Favorite Recipes

Here are some of Katie's favorite recipes that she wrote down and used a lot. Sometimes she added the name of the person who gave her the recipe:

- "Robin," of course, is Katie's second daughter.
- "Jean" is Katie's sister Jean Blanchard.
- "Gloy" is Glade's mother.
- "Alta" is the wife of Katie's brother Tom Murdoch.
- "Velda" is Velda Hill, Glade's cousin and a close family friend.
- "Harriet" is Harriet Anderson, mother-in-law to Glade's sister Connie.
- "Sadie" is Sadie Harrell, a family friend.

Poor Man's Sauce, Hot Fudge Topping

Poor Mans Sauce from Grandma Stiles for our fruit cake

Vanilla Sauce
for steamed pudding or over fruit Cake
½ C Sugar
2 T Cornstarch
¼ t salt
2 C. boiling water
4 T Butter
1 t. Vanilla
dash nutmeg
Mix & Cook till clear stirring Constantly

Hot fudge topping
1 Cube butter — don't Substitute
1 ½ C. Sugar
9 t. Cocoa
1 Can evaporated milk
Cook slowly to desired Consistency — 10-20 Min.

Chili Sauce

Chili Sauce
4 t. Whole Cloves
3 T whole Allspice
4 qts chpd. skinned ripe tomatoes 8 lbs
2 1/2 C chpd peeled onions (4)
2 1/2 C. chpd Green peppers (6)
1 1/2 C. Sugar
2 T salt
4 C Cider Vinegar

Tie spices in Cheesecloth bag. Combine remaining ingredients in kettle. Cook uncovered 2 1/2 or 3 hrs, stirring frequently. Remove spice bag. Pour into clean hot jars. Adjust Covers & process in Canner 30 min. 4 to 5 Qts.

I add sugar last it scorches so easily.

Cereal Nibbles

Cereal Nibbles
2½ C. shredded Corn biscuits
2½ C. " rice "
1 C. ready to eat oat Cereal
½ C. unsalted nuts
1 C. thin pretzel sticks
6 T. melted butter
1 t. seasoned Salt
¼ t. Garlic Salt
¼ t. Onion Salt
½ t. Celery Salt
4 t. worcestershire sauce
Oven 250°

   Combine all in a flat pan heat slowly 1 hr. stirring every 15 min. Store in Air tight jars: will keep several weeks. 8 Cups

Mustard Sauce, Maddox Dressing

Very good   *45*   *Ambrose*

Mustard Sauce   (Harriet)
½ C. dry Mustard
½ C. Vinegar
    Mix & let stand several hours.
Then add 1 egg well beaten.
⅓ C. sugar
½ t. salt
    Mix all ingredients & Place
in double boiler over hot water.
& Cook until thick. When Cool
Add 1 C. Mayonnaise — Very good
with ham

    Maddox dressing
½ C. tomato soup
¾ C. Salad oil
¼ C. Vinegar
    Mix in blender & add
1 T Onion juice
1 T worchestershire sauce
¾ t salt
½ t. dry Mustard
¼ C. sugar
Add 1 ⅓ C mayonnaise & Blend Again

Carmel Sauce, Carmel Sauce—Robin

Carmel Sauce
2 Cubes Butter
2 C. Br. Sugar
1 qt Water
2 T. Vinegar
dash Nutmeg
4 T. Cornstarch
Cook till thick

Carmel Sauce – Robin
½ C. Br. Sugar
½ C. Lt Carn Syrup
2 T. Butter
½ C. W. Sugar

Combine Bring to a boil
thicken a little if necessary.
Remove from heat +
add - 1 C. Cream
1 t. Vanilla
Do not let it boil after
Cream has been added or it
will Curdle.

French Dressing, Salad Dressing Mix (Hidden Valley)

French dressing
1 Qt. Wesson oil
1 t. Paprika
½ t. Pepper
1 C. Vinegar
1 C. Catchup
3 t. Salt
1 t. dry Mustard
1 C. sugar or less
2 T grated Onion
Blend — add oil last a little at a time.

Salad Dressing Mix (Hidden Valley)
1 t. season salt   1½ t. garlic salt
½ t. pepper   1 t. (Accent)
½ t. salt   1 t. Parsley flakes
add 2 C. Buttermilk & 2 C. salad dressing

English Toffee, Peanut Brittle

1 1/2 Tbs sugar
1 C in toffee
[at sides of kettle]

English Toffee

2 1/2 C. Sugar   1 lb. Butter
1/2 C. water   1 lb. Nuts
1/4 C. w. Karo.   1 Pkg. Choc. Chip

Boil sugar water Karo Covered to dissolve & Steam. Add butter & Cook to 280°. if Using Almonds add at 260. - Add walnuts last spread on buttered Cookie sheet - (large). Cover with Choc. Chips & spread as they Melt. Cover with gr. Nuts. Break into Pieces. Stir all the time.

Peanut Brittle

1 C. Corn syrup
1 C. water
2 C. Sugar
1 T. Butter

Cook until threads. About 248 to 260° Add 2 C raw Spanish Peanuts & Cook until light brown about 280° Add 1 t. Vanilla & 1 1/2 t. Soda. Spread thin on Buttered Cookie Sheets

Golden Fudge, Sugared Popcorn

Golden Fudge

3 C. Sugar
1/4 C. Lt. Corn syrup
3 T Butter
1/2 t. salt
1 C. evp. milk
1/2 C. water
2 t. Vanilla
Candied Cherries

Cook 1st 6 Ingredients to soft Ball - stirring several times.
Cool to 110 - Add Vanilla
Beat till smooth - spread in pan
Cut in squares. Decorate with Cherries

Sugared PopCorn

1 C. sugar
1/2 C. water
   Cook till firm Ball.
spins thread.
1 T Butter
1 t. Vanilla
   Coloring
   Stir over PopCorn till it goes to sugar.

Fudge, Pecan or Peanut Brittle

<u>Fudge -</u>   Jean.

1 2/3 C. sugar
2/3 C. Canned Milk
1/4 t. Salt
2 T Butter.

Cook stirring 5 Min., remove from heat add 6 oz pkg. Choc. Chips, 16 Marshmellows. 1/4 lb. 1 t. Vanilla 1/2 C. nuts. Beat till Melted. Pour in buttered Pan.

<u>Pecan or Peanut Brittle</u>

2 C. Sugar
1 C. nuts
1/2 t. Salt.

Melt Sugar in heavy saucepan stirring Constantly. Beat in Melted Butter, Nuts & Salt. Cool, break into Pieces.

Almond Joys, Peanut Honey Balls (Peanut Butter Cups)

Almond Joys
1 lg. pkg. flake Coconut
1 Heaping T flour
Mix — & Cook to softball
232° the following & pour
over Coconut.
⅔ C. Sugar
⅓ C. water
1 C. Corn Syrup
⅛ t. salt
Shape & put Almond on
top. Coat with Chocolate.

Peanut honey balls. (By-Peanut Butter Cups)
1 C. honey
1 C. peanut butter
1 C. powdered Milk
Mix — form into ~~balls~~
Roll into nuts.

2 Sticks melted Margarine
1¾ C. Gr. Cracker Crumbs
1 C. P.N. Butter Chunky
2½ C. ~~~~ P. Sugar
Mix & put in ~~~~ dish
cover & C. melted choc. chips 1 T. oil

Grandma's Salad

Grandma's Salad (Goop)

1 Pkg. lemon jello
1 C. hot water
Mix & cool till it starts to thicken.

Add: 12 oz. Philadelphia Cream Cheese
1 med. Can Crushed Pineapple
1 C. diced Celery
1 C. nuts
1 t. Salt
½ Pt. whipped Cream

Pour into flat Pan. Chill several hrs.

Mix 1 Pkg. red jello
1 C. hot water
1 C. Cold water

Pour over Salad Mixture & Put in frige to set.

Cranberry Salad

Cranberry Salad
3 envelopes Knox Gelatin
1/3 C. sugar
2 C. Cranberry juice Cocktail — heated
2 1/2 C. " " — cold
2 1/2 C. chpd. apple
1/3 C. " Celery
1/3 C. " Nuts

In large bowl add gelatin & sugar. Add hot juice & stir till gelatin is dissolved. Add rest of juice & chill to consistency of egg whites. Add rest & turn into 5 cup mold. Chill.

Goulash[1]

> Goulash
> 1 Angel food Cake broke in pieces.
> 1 - 12 oz. Choc. drops.
> 4 eggs.
> 1 Pt. Cream.
> 2 Heath Candy bars.
>
> Melt Choc. drops. Cool slightly.
> Add beaten egg yolks.
> Whip Cream with 3 T sugar
> & 1 t Vanilla.
> Fold into Choc. mixture.
> Crush Candy bars & add
> to mixture.
> Layer angel food Cake
> & Choc. mixture.

---

1. It's a little hard to read, but the recipe actually calls for 12 ounces (not 2 ounces) of chocolate drops (chocolate chips).

Pine Tree Salad

Christmas

Pinetree Salad
2 C. gr. Cranberries
2 Oranges 1 with peel Ground
1 C. sugar
  Mix and let stand 2 hrs.

Mix 2 Cherry Jello (3 oz)
  1 C. pineapple juice
  1 C. boiling water
  ice —
Add. 1 C. apples diced
  1 C. Celery diced
  1 C. pineapple tidbits.
Combine Cranberry Mixture
Chill Let set Several hrs..

Carrot Cake

Carrot Cake — Eva

2 C. grated Carrots
1½ C. sugar
1 C. raisins
1 C. Chpd. dates
1½ C. water
⅓ C. shortening
½ t. salt
1 t. Cinn.
1 t. nutmeg
½ t. allspice
½ t. Cloves
1 C. nuts
　Cook 5 min & Cool.
Add 2 C. flour
　1½ t. soda
　2 eggs
　Vanilla
Bake 40 min at 350°

Rhubarb Crunch

Rhubarb Crunch
4 C. Rhubarb
1 C. Sugar
2 T Corn starch
1 C. Water
1 t. Vanilla
    Cook till Clear.

1 C. flour
1 C. rolled oats
1 C. Br. Sugar
½ C. Melted butter
1 t. Vanilla
Crunch up together.
Put ½ Crunch Mixture in Pan. Cover with Rhubarb. Cover with Sauce. rest of Crunch. Bake 350° 1 hr.

Meat Loaf, Ann Landers Meatloaf[2]

Meat Loaf

- 1½ lb. gr. beef
- ½ C. br. bread Crumbs
- 1 Onion Chopped
- 1 egg
- 1½ t. salt
- ¼ t. Pepper

- 2-8 oz Cans tom. Sauce
- ½ C. water
- 3 T Vinegar
- 3 T. Br. Sugar
- 2 T. Prep. Mustard
- 2 t. Worcestershire

Mix together, beef Crumbs, egg, salt, Pepper & ½ Can of tom Sauce. Form into loaf & Put into shallow Pan. Combine rest & make Sauce & Pour over loaf. Bake 350° 1 hr. 15 Min.

Ann Landers Meat loaf

- 2 lb. gr. beef
- 2 eggs
- 1½ C. bread Crumbs
- ¾ C. Ketchup

- 1 t. Accent
- ½ C. warm water
- 1 Pkg. Onion Soup Mix

Mix – Cover with bacon & 8 oz Can tom. Sauce. Bake 350° 1 hr. Serves 6.

---

2. It's a little hard to read, but the Ann Landers meatloaf recipe says "Cover with bacon."

Applesauce Fruitcake

Nelda & Katie's
applesauce fruitcak
2 C. warm applesauce
1 C. Brandy — or 3 C. applesauce.
¼ C. Butter
½ C Lard
2 C. sugar
3 eggs
4 C. flour
4 t. soda
1 t. salt - Nutmeg & Cinn.
½ t. Cloves & allspice
   dates - Nuts + fruits
Bake 300° or 325. 1½ hrs.

Candied
1# Red Cherries Candied
1# Green Cherries Candied
1# Pineapple Candied
3 C. ?
2 C. Almonds Pecans
4 C. Walnuts
   Makes ?
   at 325° 1½ hrs.
we make 4 batches

Sweet and Sour Pork

Sweet & Sour Pork — Velda

½ c. soy sauce
2 T sherry
4 t. sugar
garlic 2 cloves
1 in ginger root
} prepare Marinade set aside

½ c. Br. sugar — heat
1 can Cranberry sauce — Mix Cornstarch
2 T Cornstarch — & Vinegar —
½ c. Cider Vinegar — Thicken
1½ c. pineapple juice
2 T Soy Sauce

2 lb. fresh pork cut in Cubes.
Cover with Cold water
heat simmer 20 min. Drain
1½ c. Veg oil
1 large onion Cut on Bias
1 lg. Celery rib "   "   "
2 Carrots "   "   "
1 in piece ginger root, sliced
5 oz Bamboo Shoots
2 t. Sesame Seeds.

Pour Marinade over Cooked pork. 1 to 3 hr.
dredge with Cornstarch fry in oil
add V. stir fry. Cover with Sweet &

Chinese Chicken and Rice Big and Little

Nilla

Chinese Chicken & Rice Big & Little
3 boneless Chicken breasts 1¾ lb.
½ lb. Mushrooms
1 Can (5 oz) Bamboo shoots
3 gr. Onions
1 stalk Celery
1 sm red pepper (opt)
1 Can Pimento (4 oz)
4 T Veg oil
¼ C. dry sherry
2 T Soy Sauce
2 T. Corn starch
1 C. Chicken Broth
2 C. Cooked Rice.

Slice Chicken thin.
Saute Chicken till it turns white.
Add Veg. Cook till tender Crisp
Blend Cornstarch & broth.
Add to Chicken stir till thick
Serve over Rice.

Snickerdoodles

Snickerdoodles
1 C. shortening
2 C. sugar
2 eggs
1/4 C. milk or applesauce
3 3/4 C. flour
1/2 t. baking soda
1/2 t. Cr. tartar   1 t. Vanilla
1/2 t. salt
1 C. chopped nuts.
Mix in order. Roll in balls & roll in cinn. sugar mixture. flatten.
Bake at 375° 10 or 11 min.

Sweet and Sour Chicken

Sweet & Sour Chicken (Sadie)

Chicken pieces —
    Soak Chicken in Salt water
wipe dry. + dip in Corn starch
+ then in beaten egg.
    Brown in oil.

Sauce —
    1/2 C. Broth
    3/4 C. Sugar
    1/3 C. Vinegar
    1/4 C. Catchup
    1 T. Soy Sauce
    Dash Salt

Heat + Thicken a little with Corn starch
Pour over Chicken in flat pan
+ Bake at 350° for 1 hr.
Baste occasionly

Sugar Cookies (Buttermilk), Cherry Delight

Sugar Cookies (Buttermilk)

- 1 C. sugar
- 1 C. Br. sugar
- ½ C. Butter
- ½ C. shortening
- 1 t. Vanilla
- ½ t. Lemon ext.
- 1 t. Nutmeg
- 3 ½ C. sifted flour
- 2 t. B. powder
- 1 t. Cr. tarter
- ¾ t. salt
- ¾ t. soda
- 1 C. Buttermilk
- sugar for tops

Mix – Bake at 400° 10 min.
425° for softer.

Cherry Delight

- 1 C. margarine
- ½ C. sugar
- ½ C. lt. Karo
- 2 egg yolks
- 2 ½ C. flour

Chill roll into Balls. dip into beaten egg whites then into 2 C. Chopped nuts. Place on cookie sheet press Candied Cherry halves in Center Bake at 325 20 min.

Filled Raisin Cookies, Pecan Diamonds

Filled Raisin Cookies
6 or 7 C. flour   2 C. Sugar
2 t. soda   1 C. Br. Sugar
1 t. salt   4 eggs
2 C. shortening   4 T Cold Water
2 t. Vanilla

Mix & roll into 2 logs freeze.

filling —
2 C. Gr. raisins   1 T flour
3/4 C. Br. sugar   1 C. water
Vanilla - nuts - butter

slice frozen dough 1/4 in thick. Put a spoon full of filling on slice - Place another slice on top will cook & seal together. Bake 375° 15 min.

(Pecan Diamonds)
1/3 C. Butter   Mix - Bake in
1/4 C. sugar   350° Oven 12 min
1 egg   9 X 9 X 2 pan
1 1/4 C. flour
_____
1/2 C. Butter   Melt Butter &
1/3 C. Br. sugar   rest of ingredients
3 T sugar   pour over 1st thing
1/3 C. Honey   Bake 350° 25 min
2 T. Cream   Cut 8 lengthwise

Pumpkin Cookies, Toll House Cookies

Pumpkin Cookies

- 2 C. Sugar
- 2 C. shortening
- 1-16 oz Can pumpkin
- 2 eggs
- 2 t. Vanilla
- 4 C. sifted flour
- 2 t. B. powder
- 1 t. soda
- 1 t. salt
- 2 t. Cinn.
- 1 t. nutmeg
- ½ t. allspice
- 2 C. Raisins
- 1 C. nuts

Mix drop from t.
Bake 350° 12 to 15 min.

Toll House Cookies

sift togeather
- 1 C + 2 T flour
- ½ t. salt
- ½ t. B. soda

Combine
- ½ C. shortening
- ½ t. Vanilla
- 6 T Sugar
- 6 T. Br. sugar
- 1 egg
- 6 oz. Choc. drops
- ½ C. nuts

Bake 375°
10 to 12 min

Pecan Tarts

Pecan tarts

Mix   ½ C. Margarine
         ½ C. sugar
Add   2 Beaten egg yolks.
         1 t. almond ext.
         2 C. sifted flour
press evenly in tart shells.
Bake 400° 8 to 10 min.

Bring to boil. ½ C. Margarine
                 ⅓ C. dk. Karo
                 1 C. P. sugar
stir in   1 C. Chopped nuts.
spoon into shells. Top with pecan half. Bake 350° 5 min.

Crunchy Bumpy Munchy Cookies (Ranger Cookies), Sour Cream Sugar Cookies

(Ranger Cookies)
Crunchy Bumpy Munchy Cookies
3/4 C. shortening   1/2 t. B. Soda
3/4 C. Br. Sugar   1 C. grated Carrot
1 egg   1 6 oz. pkg. Choc drops
1/2 C. Cider or Apple Juice 2 C. rolled Oats
1 t. Vanilla   1 1/2 C. Coconut or
1 C. flour   Crisp rice Cereal
1 t. Salt   1/2 C. raisins

Mix in order.
Spoon 2 T dough on Cookie sheet
+ flaten to 3 1/2 In. Circle. Allow 2 in. for
spreading. Bake 375° 15 min.
drizzle frosting on in spiral.
(sour Cream)?

Sour Cream Sugar Cookies
2 C. Sugar
2 eggs
1 C. Shortening
2 C. Sour Cream
Salt
nutmeg or Vanilla
2 t. soda added to Cream - Beat till foamy
Nake a soft dough. Chill.
roll + Cut Bake 350° 15 min

Rocky Road Brownies, Milk Chocolate Brownies

Rocky Road Brownies

Mix in Order.
- 1 C. Shortening
- 2 C. Sugar
- 1/3 C. Cocoa
- 4 eggs (1 at a time)
- 1 1/2 C. flour
- Salt
- 1 1/2 C. nuts
- 1 t. Vanilla

Mix & place in Greased 11 X 17 pan. Bake 25 Min at 350°. Remove from oven & Cover with Miniature Marshmellows. Return to Oven for 3 to 5 Min. Remove Cool & Frost.

Milk Choc. Brownies

- 1 - 6 oz. Choc. Chip
- 1 C. nuts
- 1 Can Sweetend Con. Milk
- 2 C. Bisqu...
- 2 T. Salad oil

Melt Choc. Add. Milk oil & Nuts. Spread in 13 X 9 X 2 pan. Bake 20 Min.

Date Spin Wheel Cookies

(Alta)

Date Spinwheel Cookies
1 C. shortening
2 C. Br. Sugar
1 t. soda
4 C. flour
½ t. Cinn.
3 eggs
Pinch salt.

Cream shortening. Add eggs. Dissolve soda in a little water & add. Add flour & Cinn. Roll out on waxed paper & spread with date filling. Roll like Jelly Roll. Chill then slice. Bake at 375°

Filling
1 lb. dates cut fine.
½ C. water
½ C. Sugar
1 t. Vanilla
½ C. nuts
¼ t. salt.

Cook until thick stirring constantly. Cool.

Molasses Sugar Cookies

Molasses Sugar Cookies

3/4 C. shortening
1 C. sugar
1/4 C. Molasses
1 egg
2 t. Baking soda
2 C. flour
1/2 t. Cloves
1/2 t. ginger
1 t. Cinn.
1/2 t. salt

Melt shortening Cool. Add sugar, Molasses & egg, beat well. Add sifted dry ingredients Roll into balls - then roll in sugar flaten slightly. Bake 375 8 to 10 Min

4 dz.

Old Cookie Cookies, Nonstick Rolled Butter Cookies

Old Cookie Cookies

½ C. Butter melted
2 C. (26) Gr. Cracker Crumbs (stale Cookies)
1 Can sweetened Condensed Milk
2 C. flaked Coconut
½ t. Vanilla
1 Pkg. Choc. drops

Mix all ingredients and pat into a greased & floured dripper pan.
Bake 350° about 20 min. don't overbake
Cool & Cut into bars.

Non stick rolled butter Cookies (Jean)

3 C. flour sifted (or less 2)
1 t. soda
2 t. Cream tarter
1 C. butter
2 eggs
salt
1 C. sugar
1 t. Vanilla

Sift dry ingredients. Cut in Butter as for pie Crust. Add rest. Roll & Cut
Bake 375° 8 to 10 min. may be formed

Chocolate Marshmallow Cookies

Chocolate Marshmellow Cookies

Cream – 1 C. sugar
½ C. shortening

Combine – 2 C. flour
½ t. soda
½ t. salt
½ C. Cocoa
1 egg
½ C. milk
½ C. nuts
1 t. Vanilla

Bake rounded spoonfuls at 350° about 10 min.

Take out & place ½ Marshmellow in Center of Cookie. Put back in oven for 2 min. Then Cool frost with Choc. frosting & a Nut on top.

Pinapple Coconut Cookies, Chocolate Chip Cookies

Pineapple Coconut Cookies

Another Recipe
Varations
Br Sugar
1 t. Vanilla
1/2 C. Raisins
3/4 C. undrained pineapple
1 t. B. Powder
1/2 t. soda

1/2 C shortening
1 C. sugar
1 egg
1/2 C. Crushed pineapple — drained
2 C. flour
1/2 t. salt
1/4 t. soda
1 1/2 C. Coconut
1/2 C. nuts

Mix & Bake 375° 12 min

Choc. Chip Cookies

1 C. shortening
1/2 C. sugar
1 C. Br. Sugar
1 t. Vanilla
2 eggs
2 C. flour
1 t. soda
1 t. Salt
1 C. nuts
2 C. Choc. Chips.   Bake at 375°

Photo Gallery

Suzanne, Jack, and Robin, about 1959.

Suzanne, Robin, and Jack with baby Kathy, 1961.

Glade, Katie, and kids on the grounds of the Mesa Temple during Gloy's mission to Arizona.

Photo Gallery

The Lyon family hits the road with their tiny Shasta trailer. Robin is looking out the back window of the blue Chevy station wagon.

Lyon family, about 1968.

Photo Gallery

151

Lyon family, about 1971.

Family (and friends) at the Point, with the kids being silly.

Photo Gallery

Katie with kids and grandkids at her parents' grave in Ashton.

Grandkids at Katie's funeral, July 23, 2018. Note the quilts on both sides. Left to right: Katie, Sally, Aaron, Scott, Cody, Ryan, Wren, Melanie, Mari, Gary, Rebekah, Johnny, Matt, Rachel, Leah, Joseph, Eric.

Photo Gallery

Remains of Murdoch home in Farnum, 2007. Photo by Jason Burt, Katie's grandson-in-law.

www.ingramcontent.com/pod-product-compliance
Lightning Source LLC
Chambersburg PA
CBHW071506040426
42444CB00008B/1520